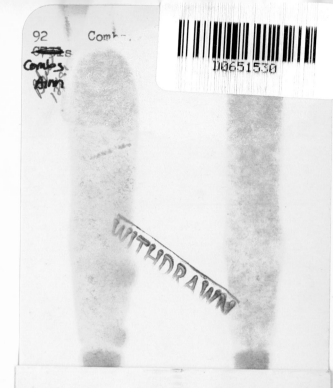

FITCHBURG PUBLIC LIBRARY

THIS BOOK IS THE PROPERTY OF THE
ABOVE LIBRARY

GOOD CARE AND PROMPT RETURN IS THE
RESPONSIBILITY OF EACH BORROWER.

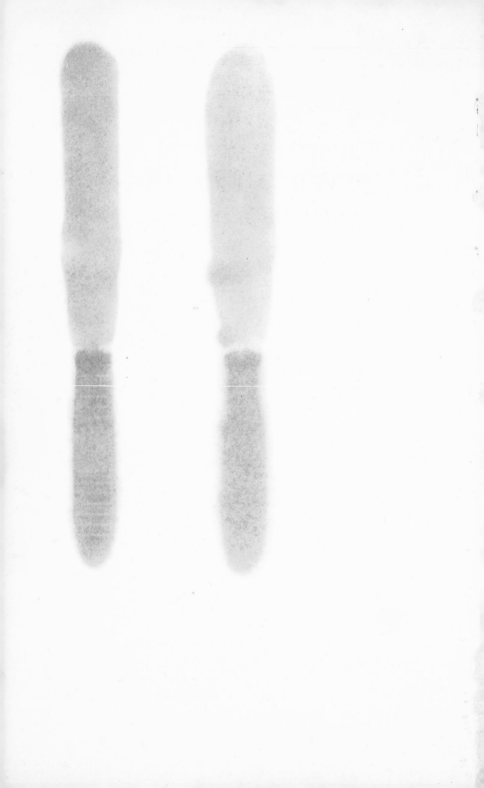

SMITH COLLEGE
NEVER TAUGHT ME
HOW TO SALUTE

1817

HARPER & ROW, PUBLISHERS, New York
Cambridge, Hagerstown, Philadelphia, San Francisco,
London, Mexico City, São Paulo, Sydney

SMITH COLLEGE NEVER TAUGHT ME HOW TO SALUTE

☆ ★ ☆ ★ ☆ ★ ☆ ★ ☆ ★ ☆

ANN COMBS

FIRST EDITION

Designer: Robin Malkin

Library of Congress Cataloging in Publication Data

Combs, Ann, 1935–
    Smith College never taught me how to salute.
    1.   United States. Air Force—Military life.
2.   Combs, Ann, 1935– 3.   Air Force wives.
I. Title.
UG633.C626   358.4′11292′0973   80–8227
ISBN 0–690–02012–0

81 82 83 84 85 10 9 8 7 6 5 4 3 2 1

To Joe
With love . . . Sir

☆ ★ ☆ CONTENTS ☆ ★ ☆

SMITH COLLEGE NEVER TAUGHT ME HOW TO SALUTE

☆ ★ ☆ 1 ☆ ★ ☆

I DON'T
RECALL ENLISTING

Smith College never taught me how to salute.

I learned about binary stars and the defraction of light. I learned to conjugate French verbs and translate Middle English. And I learned never to trust a seminarian on his way to a lifetime of celibacy. But I never learned how to salute. For though professors stressed there were no exceptions to the rule against splitting infinitives; though classmates insisted I must never wear Bermuda shorts without the mandatory knee socks; no one, not even my housemother, the resident expert on the social graces necessary for those of us trying to stumble decorously through the late 1950's, thought to take me aside and whisper, "Ann, if I were you, I'd learn how to salute."

Perhaps it was because neither she nor I nor any of the rest of those in charge of preparing us for life after Smith had considered the possibility I wouldn't follow the crowd to New York to look for a job, but would, instead, meet and fall in love with a young

1

Air Force lieutenant who'd sell me on the idea of marriage and life as a military wife.

Of course I don't know why any of us was surprised. After all I wasn't the quintessential Smith girl. I was a Westerner, an import from Washington state, where, according to rumors I helped perpetuate, Indians attacked on Wednesdays and we all caught salmon in our bare hands. Obviously someone like me who still wore jeans and went to the "movies" rather than the "flicks" would find herself, after graduation, heading down a highway other than the Merritt Parkway, New England's exit to the bright lights.

However, even I hadn't thought the highway I'd choose would lead to an Air Force base in Wichita Falls, Texas. But it had. It had gone from Smith back to Bainbridge Island, Seattle's answer to Staten Island, and then straight southeast to the plains of north central Texas, where, with 1957 only four days old, I now sat alone in a motel room, and contemplated my wedding scheduled for that evening, my future as an Air Force wife, and my total ignorance about the mechanics of saluting.

Needless to say, military greetings weren't the issue when I first met Joe Combs. It was the previous June, on a Sunday. We were in church. I, the vicar's daughter, was in the choir, a hesitant alto among thundering basses and tremulous sopranos. And Joe, in the last week of his month's leave from the Air Force, was in the congregation, wedged in the back pew between his mother and the Fogarty sisters.

I first noticed him during the sermon, when Daddy was warning the faithful about the infamous "mote in thy brother's eye." Because I'd heard the story before, and because I was a typical clergy daughter, my mind wandered before he got to the "beam" in my eye, and I scanned the congregation to see if there were any new faces.

There weren't many. The front pew, as usual, had been commandeered by the McCauleys, who were high church and fond of flaunting their synchronized genuflecting. Behind them Josh Kimball nodded off for his regular nap, and his wife, Ellie, pretended not to notice. Across the aisle were the Whitakers and their contingent of weekend guests. And several rows behind them old Mrs. Lindfelter waited patiently, the roses trembling on her lavender hat, till after the service

2

when she might accost Daddy and ask him to explain an obscure passage in Deuteronomy.

Finally I spied him there in the back, sitting ramrod straight and looking deadly serious. Say, I thought to myself, recognizing his mother and assuming the obvious, that must be Joe Combs. I wonder what he's doing here. I thought someone had told me he was married and living in Alabama.

If they had they were wrong, for Joe Combs was definitely not married. It was through no fault of his mother's. Heaven knows she'd tried. She'd introduced him to daughters of neighbors and nieces of friends. She'd pleaded with him through the mails to find a nice young girl and settle down, and whenever he came home she'd paraded the newest crop of first-round draft choices past him.

Nothing had done any good. At twenty-eight he was still a bachelor, and apparently more than content to remain so. Still, to please her he'd let her rout him out of a warm bed and drag him to church for one last look around before he headed back to his base.

I should have suspected what she was up to when later, during the coffee hour, she advanced on me much as Sherman must have advanced on Atlanta.

"Why Ann," she warbled, threading her way through groups of chatting parishioners. "How are you? I haven't seen you since last Christmas."

"Just fine," I said, noticing that even with a pained expression Joe was handsome.

"And what are you doing with yourself these days?" she went on, too casually and with too bright a smile.

"Nothing much. I just graduated, and now I'm taking the summer off."

"You just graduated, did you? Isn't that nice?" She gave Joe a knowing look, but he ignored her. "And what are your plans come fall?"

"Who knows." I shrugged. "I'm open to almost anything."

"Are you now? What do you think of that, Joe?" she asked.

I could tell what he thought of that. He thought nothing of that, and as she chattered on a hunted look came over his face. Finally he glanced at his watch and took her arm. "Come on, Mom," he said, "we'd better get going." He nodded my way. "Nice to see you," he said, and they were gone.

Well, I thought, as they headed out the door and down to the parking lot, so much for that. Too bad too. He was kinda cute.

I underestimated him. I should have realized experience had taught him to resist first and show interest later. And I should have known that after seven or eight years of practice he was an expert at seeming to avoid his mother's game plan.

But I didn't, and the next day, when he called and asked me for a date, I was surprised, and assumed his mother's clenched fist was behind the invitation.

I was wrong. The idea was his own, and, as I found out in the days following, it was an idea with considerable enthusiasm and sincerity behind it. So much so that five days later, when he caught the early ferry for Seattle and headed back to Texas, I was humming love songs, dancing impromptu gavottes, and we were unofficially engaged.

Needless to say, the news received mixed reviews. While Joe's mother was ecstatic that finally her search was over and she could relax, mine was pleased but apprehensive. While Joe's mother favored my flying down to Texas before he could change his mind and thus send her out on the trail again, mine prevailed on us to wait till Christmas, when presumably he'd be able to take another leave and come home for a proper wedding.

Mine won out through sheer perseverance. I assumed she held her ground because she wasn't totally convinced I knew what I was doing and felt I needed to take time to be sure. I also assumed, once she was persuaded that I was serious, that she had plans to put me through a crash course on the art of being a wife and home-maker.

I should have known better.

Mother was not a teacher. She was an incomparable cook. She had all the right instincts as far as dusting and mopping were concerned. She'd long since mastered the art of being a clergy wife. And as far as I knew she was a loving and sensual spouse. But she wasn't one who shared her knowledge easily.

Her patience snapped at the mere thought of me grubbing around

4

in the kitchen, slopping and stirring and neglecting to sift. Which is why at twenty-one I knew how to make a passable meat loaf, gigantic chocolate chip cookies, decorative deviled eggs complete with toothpick masts and tiny paper sails, and nothing else.

She was convinced I was beyond hope as a housekeeper, and would only learn from the time-honored tutor, experience. She knew nothing of the customs and traditions of the Air Force except that it was probably a good idea to wear gloves to all official functions. And neither of us was emotionally up to lectures and diagrams that showed "Hand A" being placed on "Thigh B."

So rather than spend the six months till Christmas in constant turmoil over when to add the egg whites, when to dust the radiator, when to call on the general, and when to get a headache, she rushed out and bought me a preparatory course for the Air Force bride-to-be. It consisted of three books: *The Kitchen Encyclopedia, The Air Force Wife,* and *Learning to Love.* She tried to find a fourth, one that would mention cleansers, sudsy ammonia, and why it's a good idea to vacuum under the bed and behind the refrigerator, but there were none. Besides the saleslady assured her *The Air Force Wife* covered the subject nicely.

I started with *Learning to Love.* It was a mistake. *Learning to Love* was not your run-of-the-mill, "Now that Dick and Jane are married, they've shut the door on Spot," type of book. The authors had done extensive research, and they were determined to let readers know they'd left no bed unturned.

One chapter dealt with a man who had a fetish for women in knickers, during a time when New York and Paris had declared them passé. Luckily he stumbled on a young lovely whose entire lower body was tattooed to look as if she were wearing a pair, and he married her immediately.

There were other chapters: a couple on romance, one on sex in old age, and one I still don't understand that advised against feeding teenagers spicy foods. There was even a section that touched on the dangers of voyeurism. "Some men," it said, "have been killed falling from roofs to which they've climbed in order to see into women's bedrooms."

I never finished *Learning to Love.*

The Kitchen Encyclopedia wasn't much better. There were 1,329 pages of alphabetically listed subjects and recipes, and each page told me more than I wanted to know.

I learned that the acacia is a thorny bush or tree, and that French chefs add acacia flowers sparingly to fritters. I read that the alewife is a fish, and that whole schools of them are often seen dead and floating on Lake Ontario. And I learned, much to my horror, how to kill a turtle before making turtle soup.

The recipes included Boned Rib Roast of Reindeer with Cranberry Stuffing, Chip Beef Pancakes, and Green Pea Soufflé. And every recipe it seemed required bouquet garni—either that or clarified butter.

I put *The Kitchen Encyclopedia* aside. Perhaps I shouldn't have, for the only volume left was *The Air Force Wife,* and if the other volumes had made me apprehensive, this one caused blind panic.

I started with the introduction, an old habit left over from school days. The author was addressing the prospective Air Force wife.

"Your fiancé will think you are something rather special," she said, "if you can listen attentively and also punctuate the conversation *occasionally* and casually with a pertinent air-minded remark."

What the devil does that mean? I thought, clenching my teeth. Am I supposed to take Joe's arm, point a gloved finger to the sky, and say, "What ho, my precious. I believe I've spotted a helicopter!"?

I flipped through more pages. "Olives should not be popped into the mouth whole," I was warned. "The flesh should be bitten away until only the stone remains."

"And what does one do with said stone?" I growled. "Does one drop it down one's front so it mayn't disgust others by sitting naked on one's plate?"

The book declined to answer, and I read on. One section covered Air Force customs and traditions. Another told about the military wedding. There was a paragraph on Quarters, another on Rank, and a third on Gun Salutes.

Then I happened on "The Masculine Bill of Rights."

1. A man has a right to man-sized chairs and to solidly built furniture.

"And where does the woman sit?" I snarled. "On burlap cushions at his feet?"

2. A man has a right to good reading lamps, large ash trays conveniently placed and a special place for his books and magazines.

"Does this idiot think wives don't read?" I snapped. "Or do we put our books and magazines in the garage, so they won't be in the way?"

3. A man has the right to a study or bedroom of his own if space permits and he wishes it. His judgment in colors should be respected.

"Don't mind me, fellow. I'll simply haul out my orange pallet, put it down here on this purple rug, and wrap myself in one of our red blankets."

4. A man has a right to privacy in his own home, and he will respect yours in turn. Do not rearrange his personal belongings. Do not use his things without asking his permission. It is said that only the greatest of souls can share fountain pens, razor blades and umbrellas with equanimity.

"My God, who am I marrying here, the Prince of Wales?"

5. A man has a right to some luxury of his own kind. He enjoys big spongy bath towels, a good light for reading in bed, a good light for shaving and a convenient place for keeping his liquor and for mixing drinks.

That did it. His liquor my foot. Living like that and I'd soon find places for my own liquor, in the linen closet, under the bed, in the oven, behind his special books and magazines. I slammed the book shut and threw it across the room.

"To hell with it," I roared.

"To hell with what?" Mother, upstairs to show me the latest additions to the wedding list, burst into the room.

"To hell with getting married and joining the Air Force."

"Oh Ann," she gasped, "surely you don't mean it."

I sighed. "No, Mother," I said, "I don't. It's just that I resent being told I'm not to use Joe's umbrella, or read his magazines, or drink his liquor. The next thing you know," I continued before she could interrupt, "I'll get a directive saying I have to wear a khaki wedding dress, march to the melodious strains of 'The Star-Spangled Banner,' and end the ceremony with a snappy salute—which, incidentally, Smith never taught me how to do."

"Don't be silly," she clucked. "This is your wedding, yours and Joe's, and the Air Force is not about to tell you what you can do at your own wedding."

I snorted. "Don't bet on it," I said. "According to *The Air Force Wife* they can do anything they damn well please."

And I was right. Not that they came at me with bolts of khaki and the sheet music for "Oh say can you see . . ." They didn't. They did, however, issue a flat "permission denied," when Joe approached them in triplicate and requested he be allowed to come north for a simple post-Christmas wedding on Bainbridge Island.

First Lieutenant Joseph R. Combs, Jr., AO3021577, they contended, was needed where he was, in the first row of classroom H26, The Photo-Radar Intelligence School, Sheppard Air Force Base, Texas. And should he be so frivolous as to want to get married, he could jolly well do it on his own time, which was any Friday night, Saturday, or Sunday.

I must say Mother took the news well. She even allowed me a few "I told you so's," and let me rant on for a bit about the course of true love being strafed and bombarded by a bunch of inconsiderate, unfeeling military types. Then, possibly because she couldn't bear the thought of having me around till spring, she suggested that if Joe couldn't come to the wedding, we'd take the wedding to Joe.

Needless to say, I more than agreed, as did he. So with an abrupt about-face we changed invitations to simple announcements, changed the date to give us time to get down there, and changed the honeymoon from a leisurely jaunt back to Texas to a hurried two days in Dallas. And early in the morning on the day after Christmas, Mother and I packed up the trousseau, the wedding presents, and the monogrammed towels, and like an itinerant band of camp followers in dyed-to-match shoes, we left for Wichita Falls and my wedding. Daddy and my brother, Geoff, nonessential for the moment, would follow later, as soon as we sounded the All Clear.

We didn't dawdle. We drove as fast as the law and our endurance would allow, and late in the evening on the twenty-ninth of December we hit the city limits and pulled in to the parking lot at the *Tumble-weed Towers,* a motel at the edge of town.

Joe was there to meet us. He'd been waiting since early afternoon, and after an exuberant greeting he took us out to a late dinner, and we dropped Mother back at the motel.

"Now don't stay out too late," she warned as she got out of the car. "We have to get an early start in the morning to organize this wedding."

According to her battle plan we had to locate a church, arrange for the reception, find a florist, get a photographer, and round up some guests.

"Oh I won't, I won't," I lied, knowing she knew I was lying. "I'll be back by eleven-thirty at the absolute latest."

Of course I wasn't. But it didn't matter. True to her word she got up at dawn, and because it was Sunday she got dressed, tiptoed past my bed, and headed out on a church inspection tour. By the time I was awake she was back with a "mission accomplished" to her credit.

"You mean you found us a church already?" I asked as she handed me a cup of instant coffee.

"That's right," she said. "Saint Mary's Episcopal Church. It's a tiny little place on Fifteenth Street, and the priest, Alden Danenbauer, couldn't have been sweeter. He said it's free on the fourth of January, that he'd be delighted to let your father take the service, and that if there's anything he and his wife Leslie can do, we're just to let them know."

"That's great," I said, "I never thought it would be this simple."

"Neither did I." She sat down on my bed and dug through her purse for her list. "But if all the other details go this well, we've got it made."

Unfortunately she spoke too soon. For while some things went smoothly, others adhered strictly to Murphy's law. The guests, for instance, were no trouble. Joe simply pleaded with his classmates, and urged them to bring a spouse or a date or both, if it wouldn't be disruptive.

Planning the reception at the Officers Open Mess was equally effortless. In fact it only took fifteen minutes. And though Mother

9

objected to the term "Open Mess" her delight at avoiding a reception at home, with its attendant hours of preparation, more than made up for her aversion to the military nomenclature.

Once that was out of the way we zeroed in on the photographer. Joe suggested we use the one on the base, a Sergeant Olmstead, who, when we routed him out of his darkroom, looked strangely like a pudgy military groundhog come out of his burrow to blink at the winter sun. Still he couldn't have been more amenable, and in the time it took Mother to say, "I want movies of the wedding and the reception for my son-in-law's parents, who won't be able to attend, and a set of black-and-white stills for a wedding book," the arrangements were made.

Locating a maid-of-honor and a best man took a little longer. When Mother and I started out from Bainbridge we'd had one of each: my cousin, Kathy, who was waiting for us to pick her up in Salem, Oregon, and Joe's friend and fellow officer, Bob Conwell. But at some point, probably as we were motoring through Chehalis, Kathy got a better offer, from a veterinarian from Coos Bay, and by the time we'd crossed the Texas state line Bob too had fled the scene. He, it seems, had been whisked away to Florida with a set of PCS (Permanent Change of Station) orders in his pocket.

This left us with a size 10, flaming red, chiffon dress, and no one to hold Joe's hand and keep him calm. I was tempted to panic, but by now Mother was on a roll. And before I could come completely unglued she'd ordered Joe to pick out a substitute from among his classmates, and had persuaded Leslie Danenbauer to volunteer to stand up for me. Luckily she didn't have to threaten the dress. It fit perfectly.

After that triumph, however, things got sticky. First there was the organist. He was not pleased with my choice of music, and my decision to replace Lohengrin and Mendelssohn with Purcell's "Trumpet Voluntary" and Handel's "Water Music."

"You can't do that," he told me.

"Why not?"

"Because Lohengrin and Mendelssohn are traditional."

"But I'm sick of them," I said. "Besides I refuse to march down the aisle with the chorus of 'Here comes the bride. Big fat and wide' ringing in my ears."

10

He shook his head and groaned, and as we walked out the door I could hear him muttering, "Why doesn't she just go ahead and have a Black Mass?"

The florist was even less cordial. Not at first, of course. When we walked into his shop he was all smiles. And when the magic word "wedding" was mentioned he positively exuded southern charm. I think he pictured a cathedral up to its narthex in stephanotis and gladioli.

Mother brought him back to earth with a thud.

"It's to be a very simple affair," she said. "All we need is two bouquets, one for my daughter here, and one for the matron of honor, and a boutonniere for my son, the acting father of the bride."

"But the altar," he drawled, giving the word more syllables than it could use. "Surely you'll need flowers on the altar."

"No. The church already has flowers on the altar."

"Perhaps a standard or two of phlox tastefully placed at the front of the church?"

Mother shook her head.

"Sprays in the windows? We have a lovely selection . . . with or without matching candles."

"No, just the bouquets and the boutonniere."

"And speaking of bouquets," I said, leaping in before he could mention rose petals, and garlands of white orchids flown in from Honolulu, "I'd like some red in my bouquet. In fact I'd like mine to be white with red, and the matron of honor's red with white."

It was as if I'd spit on the Alamo. He stared at me and swallowed so hard his string tie danced up and down. "Red?" he said. "Red? But my dear, brides wear white."

"Oh I know, but too much white is blah. I want a little color in there."

He coughed and turned to Mother. "Excuse me, ma'am. Could I speak to you privately for a moment?"

"Certainly."

They moved to the other side of the shop, and though he struggled to keep his voice low, I still could hear his horrified whispers.

"Now I don't know if you realize it," he explained as if to an

11

idiot, "but this wedding is going to be a very special time for your daughter." He paused. "It's something she'll remember forever. And though I know she thinks she wants red in her bouquet, believe me she doesn't."

"Yes she does," Mother bristled. "She's always wanted a red bouquet."

"Oh no, no, no, no, no." He took out a handkerchief and wiped his forehead. "She doesn't. She can't. If she carries a red bouquet she'll regret it for the rest of her life." He paused again. "You see," he added as if revealing the formula for Coca-Cola, "brides wear white for . . . purity."

Mother stiffened, and I pretended to be inspecting a bucket of yellow roses.

"Purity," she said in a tone I recognized as one she saved for salesgirls who call her "honey," "is not the issue. My daughter wants red in her bouquet, and I would like you to put red in her bouquet. Is that clear?"

"Oh yes, ma'am. Of course, ma'am. Anything you say." He salaamed backward into a pyramid of poinsettias marked down for post-season clearance. "Just tell me exactly when you need them, and I'll get right on it."

We did and left.

"The unmitigated nerve of that man," Mother muttered as we walked to the car. "If I had more time I'd find another florist."

"Oh Mother," I chortled, "I think it's marvelous."

"Marvelous?"

"Sure. No one's ever thought of me as impure before. I think it's neat."

Now though, two days later, with D-Day upon me, and only a few hours left before it no longer mattered whether or not the florist thought I was pure, I didn't find things so amusing. Instead, as I sat in the motel tracing the patterns on the chenille bedspread, I fluctuated between sheer terror at the thought of marriage and life in the Air Force, wistful nostalgia at the thought of leaving home, family, and my old rag doll, Heidi, a sense of regret because now I'd never have my own apartment and live the carefree life of a single girl, a feeling of inadequacy because my homemaking skills

12

were negligible, and a wild exhilaration at the thought of what lay ahead. It was exhausting, and after an hour or so, I gave up, took a shower, painted my toenails, and waited for everyone to come back from the tour of the city so we could go out to dinner and get that over with.

The time on the invitations said 8:30 P.M. Informal photographs were scheduled for earlier. Mother decreed they would be segregated, with me in the warmth and comfort of the vicarage, and Joe and Art Winters, his best man, relegated to the sacristy, where vestments and choir robes precluded hilarity and encouraged Joe's nervousness.

Sergeant Olmstead came to me first. Out of his uniform, he now looked like a civilian groundhog. Light meters and flash bulbs peered out of his pockets. Cameras hung around his neck, and under his arm he carried a tripod.

While Leslie and Mother and I had a cup of coffee he scampered around the room arranging lights and assessing backdrops. Then the session began. I stood. I sat. I smiled. I laughed. I took my veil off. I put it on again. I held my red and white bouquet, and tried to look pure. I tossed it to Leslie, and tried to look impure.

Finally, with one last, "Now smile," he doused the lights, gathered up his equipment and clattered off to search out Joe. We let him go, and after a few minutes I put my veil back on again, and we too headed over to the church.

We shouldn't have waited. Sergeant Olmstead, it seems, was a frustrated movie producer and in the time it had taken us to drink one last cup of coffee, he'd managed to set up enough equipment to film *Gone With The Wind*.

In fact the entire left side of the church, with the exception of the front pew, where Mother stood trying desperately not to look as if she were a Speed-Graphic salesman, was filled with Nikons, Leicas, and Hasselblads. Cords were hanging, draped from one pew to the other like the garlands the florist would have suggested, and packs of film were strewn along the pews. Across the aisle what congregation there was huddled together like refugees in an over-loaded life boat.

Joe stood in front of the altar with Art and Daddy. He didn't look well. His face was ashen, and I could see his hands shaking.

13

All he needed was a set of handcuffs and the warden.

As the organist launched reluctantly into the "Trumpet Voluntary," I took Geoff's arm.

"Let's go," I whispered. "I think Joe's about to bolt."

"OK," he said, and we started down the aisle.

Fifteen minutes later, after a few shaky "I do's" and "I will's" and a sobering "till death us do part," we were married.

As promised, Sergeant Olmstead got the whole ceremony on film. Unfortunately his skill did not match his enthusiasm—it was all from the waist down.

By the time he got to the reception, however, he'd recovered his equilibrium. In fact we all had. My hands were no longer cold and clammy. Joe was smiling. He even had some color in his face. True, it disappeared for a spell when, after forty-five minutes of waiting, we learned that the guard was holding Mother, Daddy, Geoff, and the Danenbauers at the main gate because they had no passes. But he settled that in a hurry with one scorching phone call, and the roses returned to his cheeks.

After the first glass of punch everyone loosened up a bit. Daddy and Alden Danenbauer compared liturgical notes. Mother and Leslie compared Ladies' Auxiliary horror stories. Geoff and Art discussed obsolete aircraft. Joe introduced me to the other men and their wives, and Lieutenant Bristol's wife, Carrie, awash with fervent sincerity, complimented me on everything from the music to the color of my eyes.

"And most of all I love your bouquet," she gushed. "Why my stars and garters, isn't it just too perfect to have a bit of color. As I told Clark, if I were doing it again, I'd have a bouquet just like yours."

Sergeant Olmstead, primed with punch, scurried about orchestrating memorable shots.

"That's right, ma'am. Feed Lieutenant Combs the first bite of cake."

"Good idea. Give your bride a kiss."

When it came to throwing the bouquet, and I kicked off my shoes so I could stand on a chair, he went into a frenzy.

"Oh that's marvelous. The shoes are the perfect touch."

I think he had a foot fetish.

By 11:00 it was over. The punch bowl was empty. The cake had been eaten. The candles were burned down, and most of the guests had trilled their final congratulations and left.

One last ritual remained—the grand exit for the honeymoon. Custom and Mother dictated a change to a traveling costume. But the club had no dressing rooms. So we all journeyed back to the motel.

It would be a simple matter, or so I thought. Off with the old, on with the new, and out the door in a shower of rice. I was wrong. Like actors after an opening-night performance, everyone wanted to sit for a while and discuss their parts.

So while I changed clothes Geoff brought out a bottle of Scotch, Joe went down the hall for some ice, Mother took off her shoes and massaged her feet, and Daddy sat back in his chair and regaled everyone with his and Mother's first fight.

I didn't take long at all. In five minutes I was ready to go. But still we stayed. Ten minutes later I cleared my throat. I was ignored. Five more and I headed for the door, but Daddy was up to the time when Mother broke all of her phonograph records over his head, and Joe shushed me.

Finally there was a pause.

"Anyone for a rubber of bridge?" I asked.

Joe leapt to his feet. "Oh Lord," he said, "we're supposed to be on our honeymoon, aren't we?"

"Yes, Sir." I snapped to attention and, though Smith hadn't taught me how, I faked a salute.

Minutes later we were on our way.

15

☆ ★ ☆ **2** ☆ ★ ☆

PULL UP A HUNK
OF TUMBLEWEED ...
YOU'RE HOME

It's my own theory of course, but I suspect when God was making Wichita Falls, His mind was on something else. Perhaps He was congratulating Himself on Santa Fe, or worrying for fear He'd put Denver up too high. Whatever it was, He wasn't paying attention to the task on hand, for if He had He would have realized the error of His ways and decided instead to make another purple mountain majesty or perhaps an amber wave of grain.

The city of Wichita Falls, the county seat of Wichita County, lies on the northern plains of Texas, in the famed Red River valley. It's east of Harrold, west of Henrietta, northwest of Joy, and about thirty miles south of Cookietown, Oklahoma. The plains around the city are classified as rolling. Translated this means if you're driving in from Amarillo with the summer sun blistering the paint off your car, and your steering wheel locked into automatic pilot because it's been two hours since you had to turn it more than one quarter of an inch, you'll look ahead, see a hill, and say, "There's got to be something on the other side of that." The something will turn out to be another twenty-mile stretch of road and another far hill. Wichita Falls is an odd sort of town. New Englanders have never heard of it. Folks from Montana think it's a city in Kansas. Meteorologists call it the center lane in Tornado Alley, and fellow Texans apologize for it, saying, "Now don't y'all judge the whole state by Wichita Falls. The rest of Texas is lovely."

My first impressions, however, were all favorable. Of course I was in love at the time. Therefore, in the same spirit one first meets one's prospective in-laws, I was willing to believe the best.

I'd already boned up on the pertinent facts about Wichita Falls. I knew, for instance, that it was founded in 1876 by John Scott. And I knew he'd chosen a site that thirty-five years earlier had been a Wichita Indian village. Had I not been so naive and trusting, I might have thought to ask why the Wichita Indians decided to leave.

I'd read that 1918 was a big year in the history of the city; 1918 was the year they struck oil. I knew that in the late '20s Wichita Falls gained fame as being the home of the longest stretch of paved concrete in the state of Texas; that *Boomtown,* starring Clark Gable and Spencer Tracy, had been filmed "up the road a piece" in Burkburnett; that Wichita Falls was the home of the State Mental Hospital; that shooting firecrackers was a traditional way to celebrate Christmas, Easter, Millard Fillmore's birthday, and any other holiday that happened to be hanging on the calendar at the time; and that the city had more millionaires per capita than any other in the United States. Finally I learned that Sheppard Air Force Base, my home to be, was built about the same time nylon stockings first went on sale.

That was my history lesson. The statistical information I'd been given led me to believe I was about to take up residence in the most ideal setting east of Santa Barbara, California. After all, who could ask for more than to be in a town where the skies are blue, the average temperature is 64 degrees, and there are only 27 inches of rain in a year?

Who can resist a town that boasts 130 churches, twenty-some schools, a university, a beauty college, two newspapers, eight theaters,

17

numerous restaurants, modern motels, a symphony orchestra, "round" dance clubs, fishing, boating, golfing, bowling, swimming, skiing, and year-round "varmit" hunting?

Of course after a while the wheat would emerge from all the chaff, and I'd learn that when the skies weren't blue they were red, as storms whistled over the plains and blew dust in around the windows and under the door. I'd learn that one averages a temperature by taking the 12 degrees on January 16, the 74 degrees on January 17, the 112 degrees on July 9, adding them to the other extremes of heat and cold, then dividing by 365.

This was somewhat of a shock to me. Being from the Pacific Northwest, where the temperature varies slightly and only in direct proportion to the thickness of the cloud cover, I'd imagined I'd be wallowing in day after day of warm caressing sunlight and a year-round tan, not frostbite and four-blanket nights.

"I thought this was the South," I said to our landlady one day as I was chipping ice off the inside of the living room window. "And I thought the South was supposed to be subtropical."

She laughed. "Honey," she said, "this ain't anywhere. This is Wichita Falls, and once you've lived here awhile you'll realize what they say is true. In winter there's a barbed wire fence between Wichita Falls and the North Pole, and it's down. In summer there's a screen door between here and hell, and it's open."

She was right, and I suspect it was the wind that blew the fence down and kept the screen door open, for the wind blew constantly. It was like living in the prop wash of a departing helicopter. Hats were never worn unless you had a hand free to clamp them to your head. Skirts billowed and whipped around your knees and wore out from the sheer exhaustion of it. And giant balls of tumbleweed bounced and skittered across the landscape heading for Arkansas and points east.

Of course the brochures Joe'd sent me had never mentioned the wind. But then I soon discovered that they, like a doting grandmother, were not always strict purveyors of the truth. Not that they lied. They didn't. There actually were 130 churches. I checked in the phone book one day and counted them just to be sure. Some, however, judging from their designations as "new," "reorganized," and "non-affiliated," had, I suspect, clerics with mail order divinity degrees.

There were also two newspapers: the *Times* and the *Record News*. The same man owned both, though, and like identical twins one had trouble telling them apart.

It certainly had an adequate number of schools, in all categories; and Midwestern University would later boast Senator John Tower as one of its former faculty members.

But in the world of entertainment things were definitely limited, for Wichita Falls was not a frequent stop for touring entertainers or traveling Broadway shows. It could have been. Dallas and Oklahoma City weren't so far away that side trips to the outback couldn't have been arranged. But it hardly seemed worth it.

When Victor Jory came to town as Big Daddy in *Cat on a Hot Tin Roof* and stormed across the stage bellowing, "Crap," ladies in the front row fainted, and those on the aisle rushed outside for air.

Even Louis Armstrong, America's musical ambassador to the world, was greeted by only a lethargic few.

Local television was fun though, especially the newscasts. I never missed one if I could help it. They always had a delicious element of surprise. Was the weatherman going to break up on camera when his temperature charts slid off the easel and sailed across the room? Would the anchorman make it through without mispronouncing Khrushchev or parapsychology? Would the film of the warehouse fire get mixed up with the report on the beauty contest, leaving the announcer with nothing but a mouthful of non sequiturs?

I could hardly wait for evening to come, to see if once again the cameraman's obscene gesture to the sports announcer would be shadowed and magnified forty times over on the backdrop wall.

Election years were particularly exciting with their television fare. There was none of this "Let my worthy opponent come forward and explain his voting record," or "I beg to differ with his stand on urban renewal." Candidates got right to the heart of the matter.

"Moses gave us the Ten Commandments," I once heard a man running for sheriff say, "and my opponent, Jimmy Jay Boyd, has broken each and every one of them."

He then went on to elaborate, and for half an hour I sat riveted to my chair listening as he counted them off. Luckily for Jimmy Jay, numbers six and seven (murder and adultery) were more symbolic than actual. Luckily too the voters didn't seem to care. I later checked the election returns. Jimmy Jay won—by a landslide.

An alternative to television or Cecil B. De Mille's latest biblical epic at a local theater was dinner out. Here too I was led astray by claims of "down South hospitality," and "succulent cuisine for every palate."

It all depended on whether or not one's palate craved ribs, hush puppies, and black-eyed peas. If it did the doors of Hy's Hikry Pit and El Gaucho's Bar "B" Q were always open. If not it was best to settle for a steak and baked potato at home, or try the lasagna at Testes Italian Restaurant on the Sheppard Access Road.

The most flagrant bit of distorted advertising, however, lay in the claim that Wichita Falls was a recreational Mecca. According to the brochure, hunting, fishing, boating, golfing, swimming, skiing, and bird watching were all available. On reading the fine print I discovered that "available" depended on how far you are willing to travel. Deep sea fishing, for instance, was "available"—off the Gulf Coast. All you needed was a free weekend and a round-trip ticket out of the Municipal Airport. Hunting was "available"—in the mountains of Colorado. And bird watching was certainly "available" in San Antonio or Santa Fe. One could even indulge in the fine old sport of rattlesnake sacking if he liked. But not in Wichita Falls. For that you had to go to Austin.

Locally you could bowl. You could watch the ducks on Lake Wichita, or you could try and find out whatever happened to Wichita's falls, but not a lot else.

But then I was a recreational snob. Coming as I did from an area where you could look out your front window and watch the salmon jumping out of the water, I was spoiled. To me skiing was a half hour's drive to 6,000 feet and dry powder. Boating was two weeks of cruising in the San Juan Islands, or maybe an afternoon of rowing in Port Blakely Bay. And swimming was running down to the beach in front of our house and wading into the icy waters of Puget Sound.

I refused to believe anyone could enjoy less. I was wrong as usual. One day in line at the bank I happened to overhear two men making extensive plans for a fishing trip.

I wonder where they're going, I thought as they batted fishing terms back and forth like Ping-Pong balls at a championship match. Maybe they're headed over to New Mexico looking for trout. Or they might be going down to Houston or Galveston.

The line moved up to the teller's cage and I moved with it, eavesdropping all the way.

"Why hi there, Mr. Shelton," the teller said as the first man took out his deposit slip and a handful of checks. "You two going fishing again this weekend?"

"Sure are, Mildred," he said.

"Mah stars," she said, "where are you going this time, Lake Texarkana?"

"Nope. There's lots better fishing here at home—in the drainage ditch on the outskirts of town."

It was probably a drainage ditch out by the base, for Sheppard was certainly on the outskirts of town, two miles to the north in fact. It was like a children's wing added onto a house. You put it close enough to let you keep an eye on the little ruffians, but kept it far enough away so they wouldn't mix a lot with the grownups.

Originally built in 1940, Sheppard had been a basic training center during the Second World War. After the war it was deactivated. Then in 1948 it was activated again.

At first I assumed all this shifting back and forth—putting up, taking down, activating, and deactivating—was the reason the base looked as if it could be dismantled and loaded onto a flatbed truck at a moment's notice. I was wrong. I later learned all Air Force bases look this way.

Apparently military tradition dictates that when it's time to throw up another base, a group of generals and full colonels gather together in a subterranean room in the Pentagon and draw up the plans.

"All right," the ranking officer says, "Sergeant Gustafson will hand out pencils, paper, and a ruler for each of you. The first thing I want you to do is draw a grid." (They like grids in the Air Force. It helps them find their targets.)

21

Once the grids are drawn, they all write "North" at the top of the paper, and that's a new base. Of course there's some discussion as to what to name the streets. And because they're all career officers, and have been in the service for at least fifteen or twenty years, they argue a while, cite military directives, and finally settle on "First," "Second," and "Third," for those running north and south, and "A," "B," and "C," for those going east and west.

Later, when they're plotting the housing area, they get silly and capricious and name the lanes and boulevards after rockets and missiles, and other sentimental explosives.

This completed, they call for the sergeant again and tell him to bring in the standard *Air Force Base* kit. It's like a bag of building blocks. It comes with a commissary, a base exchange, a hospital, a clothing store, headquarters, a whole fistful of barracks, the commander's quarters, a couple of mess halls, an Air Police headquarters, the NCO club, the enlisted men's club, and the officers' mess. Everyone takes a turn placing a block.

"I get to put the BX here."

"All right, but I get to put the barracks over here, near the end of the runway."

"How about if I combine the beauty shop and the bowling alley and stick them next to the BX?"

"No, no, that's too easy. Put them over by the hospital."

And so it goes. The game continues till five, when they quickly scatter whatever is left and all adjourn to the officers' mess for a couple of martinis.

Sergeant Gustafson gets to gather up the pencils and papers and type the orders. Then just before he turns out the lights and heads for home he pushes the "activate" button and another base is born.

The actual construction offers no surprises. All the buildings are long, low, wooden, and the color of evaporated milk. They're all placed the same distance from the sidewalk. They're all surrounded by closely cropped crabgrass. And they're all tagged with a letter and a number so the inspection team won't get lost and check one barracks twice.

Sheppard, of course, followed the pattern to the final carbon copy. And it adhered to the standard prototype in that it had been plunked down next to a town that looked out its back door in horror one morning, and said, "Oh, my God, Martha, an Air Force base. Well there goes the neighborhood."

I don't know why they were so upset. After all, we balanced out the population. Without the military, Wichita Falls had only two groups of citizens: the very rich and the very poor. It was easy to tell them apart. The very rich wore torn jeans and muddy cowboy boots, and looked as if they'd been left as living donations for the Goodwill truck.

The very poor were neat and pressed, and worked two jobs to try and make ends meet.

In the middle, barely tolerated by the one faction and openly hated by the other, was the military.

And in the middle of the military, standing with her thumb in her mouth like the new kid in school waiting to find out which locker was hers, was I, Ann Combs, housewife second class, about to begin OJT (on the job training).

☆ ★ ☆ **3** ☆ ★ ☆

SETTLE DOWN, TROOPS

According to *The Air Force Wife,* the typical honeymoon for the young bride marrying into the military consists of "a motor trip through New England or the Smokies in the autumn, concluding with a gay visit in New York attending the theater and a round of night spots."

Obviously, *The Air Force Wife* never attended Photo-Radar Intelligence School at Sheppard. For when Joe brought up the subject of honeymoons, he was given permission to stand at ease from Friday afternoon till Monday morning at six, no more.

This left us with a motor trip that extended to Dallas and no farther. Normally this would have been fine. After all, Dallas had Neiman Marcus and the zoo. It had shops. It had bookstores. And I assume it also had its share of theaters and night spots. But Joe was anxious to get back. He'd been a bachelor, with its attendant frivolity, for seven years, and he was ready to settle down—now, immediately—without further ado.

I prevailed on him not to head back Saturday night, using unmilitary tactics and a filmy pink and black creation to persuade him further. He agreed it was a long drive and a bit late for starting out. When Sunday morning woke and yawned and stretched, however, he issued the travel orders. So we leapt up, had a hurried breakfast, and headed back to Wichita Falls.

We pulled up in front of the apartment shortly after noon. It was a garage apartment: four rooms and a bath snuggled up to one side of our landlord's garage. The view, if one could call it that, was less than scenic. The living room, kitchen, and bath looked out at the back of the Mackies' house and Mrs. Mackie's clothesline. The vista from the dining room and the bedroom was an alley.

Mr. Mackie had built the apartment himself. He'd made the kitchen cupboards. He'd put up bookcases in the living room. He'd constructed an elaborate dresser, bureau, night table, and bed complex that extended along two walls of the bedroom. I think his interest waned, however, when he came to the bed. Either that or his supply of lumber dwindled. For the slats barely reached from one side to the other, and sometimes in the middle of the night they shifted, and the whole contraption—box spring, mattress, and all—collapsed like a spent soufflé.

Mrs. Mackie, however, was responsible for the furnishings. Not that she had an advanced degree in upholstering, or because she was an apprentice cabinetmaker. She'd won everything. She was a graduate of the Gwinnett School of Contests, and all the major appliances were either first or second prizes in one contest or another.

She'd acquired the refrigerator by coming up with a statement in 25 words or less that praised the silken sudsiness of a liquid dishwashing soap. The stove she got through the courtesy of a "Name the Zinnia" contest, and the dining room table and chairs—a vision of Formica, vinyl upholstery, and simulated brass—were the result of guessing how many jelly beans were in a five-gallon jar.

Where she got the paper draperies I'm not sure. Perhaps they were thrown in as a bonus when she won the pony they stabled for a while in our joint yard.

The main entrance to the apartment was through the back door into the kitchen. Of course we could have used the living room front door. After all they were both on the same side of the house. But the back door was closer to the street.

The kitchen was classified as a pullman kitchen. Now that I think of it, the bathroom, inconveniently placed in what must have been a converted broom closet to the left of the door, looked like a pullman bathroom too. In fact the whole apartment could easily have been fitted with an engine and a caboose and sent out of town on rails, and no one would have noticed the difference.

The kitchen was dark. Mr. Mackie, obviously not an interior decorator, had painted it a deep blue, with watermelon red counters and a black speckled floor. The only window was a pane of glass in the back door, and it was curtained. Even at high noon on a cloudless day with all the lights blazing, it was like fixing lunch in a tunnel. But in my newlywed euphoria I chose to think of it as cozy.

The bathroom was not cozy. It was small, period. It had a tub that looked as if it belonged to someone's miniature collection. It was so short, even I had to assume the fetal position in order to fit in it. A sink, a toilet, and a water heater filled out the complement of fixtures; and all four, wedged together like dishes in a packing crate, rocked on an undulating floor that apparently had buckled during a previous plumbing disaster.

The dining room was off the other end of the kitchen. The refrigerator lived in the dining room. There certainly wasn't any room for it in the kitchen. There wasn't much room for it in the dining room either, but it was that or a trip to the bedroom every time I needed an egg or a head of cabbage.

Had Joe been marching the troops through the apartment on an inspection tour, he would have ordered a "left face" in the dining room and a "forward march" to the tiny hallway. Another "forward march" would have put the boys in our bedroom, while a "left face" would have sent them clattering into the living room. It would have been a short tour, twenty steps in all.

Two walls of the living room were paneled in imitation knotty pine. The other two were papered in a gray and pink historic-scenes-from-our-nation's-past pattern. The couch was a west Texas brown, and the one upholstered chair was a dusty rose. The entire room gave one the impression he'd just stumbled into a dude ranch in Williamsburg, Virginia.

Joe and I had already moved in my belongings before the wedding. So when we came back from Dallas, towels already hung in the bathroom, the kitchen cupboards were already filled with new dishes, six of everything in "Springtime Sunrise," and pots and pans that would never be as shiny again. And the bookcase in the living room looked like a lending library for a liberal arts major. The bed was already made up. My drawers were already filled with blouses, lingerie, gloves to match every outfit, and an assortment of heady colognes.

In time the clothes, hanging pristine and separated in the closet, would jumble and mix together—my suit next to Joe's raincoat, his uniforms next to my dresses. Soon his pliers and the Phillips screwdriver would mingle in the utensil drawer with the spatula and the butter curler. And the medicine cabinet would become a mixture of shaving cream and scented bath oil, mascara and razor blades. But for the time being it was early newlywed all the way—neat, orderly, and divided.

The Mackies were just coming back from church when we drove up.

"Mah stars," Mrs. Mackie said as Joe parked the car and we got out, "y'all sure did come back early."

She was a tall slender woman with blond hair streaked by years of Texas sunlight, and a complexion that seemed to be in a state of permanent tan. Her drawl, later identified as being a dialect of west Texas, was like slow honey. One sentence and you could feel sultry summer days so hot and still that even conversation was a chore.

Mr. Mackie was tall too, but dark and animated. Unlike his wife, who moved languidly, he was always busy. If he wasn't tinkering with their car, a 1955 Ford Mrs. Mackie had won with a four-line poem about toothpaste, he was pruning shrubbery or repainting a back bedroom.

"Oh, I needed to finish unpacking," I stuttered, explaining our premature arrival. "Besides, Joe has to be back at class at six tomorrow morning."

My reason didn't make any sense, but I was flustered. I was fully aware that honeymooners are purported to spend most of their time in varying stages of connubial bliss. But according to the dictates of my British heritage, I should never admit I indulged in anything more frolicsome than high tea. So I was anxious to dispel the notion Joe and I had hurried home to cavort under the comforter.

I needn't have bothered. She accepted my explanation without comment and went on into her house.

Joe accepted my explanation too. We'd left a couple of cartons in the living room, and he brightened visibly when he heard me say I had to finish unpacking. I think it was part of his compulsion to settle down. As long as one box remained taped shut he didn't consider the marriage legal.

He did help me though, and together we put away aprons, table-cloths, and dish towels that wished us long life and perpetual sunshine in Swedish. We also moved the box for Joe's cat, Felicia, out of the bedroom and into one corner of the dining room. It wasn't that I didn't like Felicia. I simply didn't want to wake up staring into her furry face every morning. Joe had adopted her when he first moved in and was alone and lonely. She was gray and white and looked as if at one point a Persian had tiptoed through her ancestry, and she was not pleased with the new living room arrangement.

"Too bad, Felicia," I told her as I lifted her off the bed for the third time in a row, "but you have been replaced."

Late in the afternoon I geared myself up to cook my first dinner. I could hardly wait. I had the menu firmly in mind. It consisted of everything I knew how to cook, except for the deviled eggs and cookies of course.

First there would be meat loaf. I'd use Mother's recipe. She'd already written it down on a three-by-five card and put it in a yellow recipe box she'd given me. For starch, and I knew each meal must have its starch, I'd have baked potatoes. (Scrub well and grease the outside with margarine.) The vegetable would be a salad. Nothing fancy, just lettuce, tomatoes, sliced cucumbers, and a green onion, with a dollop of mayonnaise on top. I liked the sound of the word dollop. It smacked of French cuisine.

Apple pie was scheduled for dessert. I was good at making apple pies. In fact it was the only thing I'd ever done well in eighth-grade Home Ec.

I'd make the meat loaf first. I got out my new green bowl, my new bread pans, my new chopping bowl, my new chopper, my new hamburger, my new tomato sauce, and my new onion. My, this was fun. The house was warm and cozy. I could hear the television mumbling in the living room and the sound of Joe thumbing through the Sunday paper.

I put on an apron and checked the recipe to be sure I had everything out.

"Anything I can do to help?" Joe said as he came in to make us a drink.

"No, no, you just relax." I thought a minute. "Unless of course you could help me figure out something."

"Sure." He handed me a drink and put his down on the drainboard. "What do you need to know?"

"Well it's logistics. According to this recipe, I have to bake the meat loaf at three hundred degrees for two hours; the potatoes, however, are supposed to cook for one hour at three seventy-five. And though the pie only takes an hour to bake too, it needs a temperature of four twenty-five. What do I do?"

"Let's see." Joe took out a pencil and hunted up a piece of paper. He scribbled for a minute. "OK, I think I have it," he said. "Bake the pie first, then the meat loaf and potatoes together. I know the potatoes are supposed to have more heat, but the longer cooking time should make up for it."

"All right," I said, "that's what I'll do."

I put away my new green bowl, my new bread pans, my new chopping bowl etc. and I got out my new red bowl, my new pie pan, my new shortening, my new flour sifter, and the rest of the apple pie paraphernalia.

"Wait a minute," Joe said as I got out my old pie recipe. "It's four o'clock now. Let's say it takes half an hour to make the pie. Then an hour more to cook. That will make it ready around five-thirty. So if the meat loaf takes two hours more, it'll be seven-thirty before we can eat. Isn't that a bit late?"

"Oh—you're right." I looked around. "Say," I said, "maybe I can find another apple dessert as long as I have the apples." I flipped through my cookbook. "Here's one—Crusty Baked Apples. They only take half an hour, and they're probably easier to make anyway. If we have them we could eat around six forty-five. Is that all right?"

"Sure." Joe picked up his drink and headed back to the living room, where the last of an ice hockey game waited on the TV.

"Oh, wait a minute," I called. "It says here that Crusty Baked Apples have to be served with Fluffy Sauce, and Fluffy Sauce calls for vanilla and powdered sugar. We don't have either."

"Oh—well—what else is there?"

"I don't know. Let me look." I turned to the apple section again. There were four pages of recipes. There were apple turnovers, but they called for puff pastry and I had a feeling that was beyond me. Next was applesauce cake. Cancel that. It meant making applesauce first. Apple Crumble looked encouraging till I saw it required rolled oats. Panic was rising in my throat like water in a tub. Finally I hit on an idea.

"Why don't we simply have sliced apples and cheese?" I said. "That would save a whole hour and a half—or is it forty-five minutes?"

There was a silence. Joe put his drink down again. "Apples and cheese?" he said. "Just plain? For dessert?"

"Sure, it's good."

"I don't know. We never had just plain apples and cheese at our house."

"Well then, now's a good time to try them."

Joe raked his fingers through his hair. Then his face brightened. "I tell you what," he said. "Why don't we skip dessert? It's getting late, and I could stand to lose some weight anyway."

Boy, he certainly is picky, I thought. Just because he never had apples and cheese at home is no reason not to try them. I wondered what had happened to the receptive fellow who told me anything I wanted was all right with him.

"OK," I muttered, "no dessert." And I put away my new red bowl, my new pie pan, my new shortening, and my new flour sifter. I then got out the green bowl again. By now it was aging rapidly.

Joe hovered around nervously. "Is there anything else I can do?" he said.

"No, no." My martyr's cloak was firmly in place. "You just relax."

"Are you sure I can't help?"

"I'm positive. Just take your drink and go on in and watch the news or something."

He shrugged. "Well . . . if you're sure."

"I am. Now go."

He went.

He could have asked one more time, I thought. After all, the onions have to be chopped, and he could open up the tomato sauce. I banged around the kitchen slamming cupboard doors and rattling pots.

"Are you all right?" he called from the other room. I think he was scared to come in and see.

"I'm fine." My voice sounded like a typewriter clicking with self-righteousness. "Just fine."

"Yes, sir," I muttered under my breath, "I'm just fine. If you can't see I need help," I continued with my own peculiar logic, "I'm certainly not about to point it out to you. Now where are those damn bread pans?"

By eight-fifteen I had dinner on the table, and my demeanor had changed. It hadn't improved, only changed. Now I was cloying with apologies for everything from the lateness of the hour to the absence of the salt and pepper shakers on the table. I think I was waiting for absolution, for assurances that my behavior, which even I recognized as being bizarre, was forgiven.

Poor Joe. All this was new to him, and he had the look of someone suddenly plunked into the middle of a bad dream. Luckily, though, once we'd eaten and had a glass or two of wine, we both relaxed. I stopped babbling, and he smoothed the feathers he hadn't remembered ruffling.

By the time we'd finished and the dishes were done, it was late.

"Come on, honey," Joe said, turning off the kitchen light, "let's go to bed."

It was fine with me. I'd had enough of playing house. As far as I was concerned it was time to get back to the pampered world of

31

being a bride before the gossamer wings disintegrated permanently.

"I'll be right there," I told him, "as soon as I've washed my face and brushed my teeth."

"OK."

He was winding the clock when I came into the bedroom. "I'm setting this for five," he said. "That way I have time to bathe, shave, get some breakfast, and still be in class by six."

I made a face. "Sounds awfully early to me," I said. "Is this what they mean by the honeymoon being over?"

He put the clock down and leered at me. "Not in the least, my little pet. The honeymoon will be over when I tell you it is and not a minute before. Now come here and I'll explain."

I soon forgot dinner had taken forever to get ready, that Joe didn't want apples and cheese, and that the meat loaf pans were still soaking in the sink.

The next thing I knew, the alarm was ringing.

"Oh, no," I groaned, "it can't be morning already."

Joe jumped out of bed. "Don't worry, honey," he said. "Stay there. You don't have to get up. I can get my own breakfast."

I was tempted, but I knew what happens to wives who neglect their husbands and sleep in. Mother and *The Air Force Wife* had made it perfectly clear. The next thing they know they're padding around the house in bathrobe and curlers till noon. Then they start watching game shows and soap operas. They consume whole cartons of bonbons in one sitting. They put off the laundry for days at a time. They leave greasy plates and half-full cereal bowls on the table till four. In the end their husbands leave them for someone who irons underwear and vacuums out the fireplace every week.

I leapt out of bed. "No, no, I'll get your breakfast. Don't worry. I'm good at breakfasts. They're my specialty. How about bacon and eggs?"

"Fine." He disappeared into the bathroom. I slipped into my peignoir. It was a smoky pink chiffon trimmed in black feathers; not exactly my type, but the saleslady had insisted that corduroy before the second year was asking for trouble.

I put on some bacon and started the coffee.

"Only one egg for me," Joe called out. "I'm not very hungry."

"OK." I was having trouble keeping my sleeves out of the pan, and every now and then a feather floated in with the bacon. By the time he was dressed and ready I had breakfast on the table.

"Did you bring in the paper already?" Joe asked as he opened the back door and looked out.

"No."

"Oh." He sat down and I filled his coffee cup. "I guess he's late again."

"I guess so."

We ate in silence. Then Joe pushed his chair back. "Well," he said, "I guess I'd better be going." He looked at his watch. "Say, what time do you have? I must have forgotten to wind this thing again."

I pushed the chiffon and feathers aside. "I don't know," I said. "Mine seems to have stopped too. I have twelve-thirty."

"Twelve-thirty? That's what I have." He got up and went into the bedroom. He came back with the clock in his hand. It too said twelve-thirty.

Joe grinned. "We seem to have gotten up rather early," he said.

"You mean it actually is twelve-thirty?"

"Looks like it"—he laughed—"but just think. Now you can legally sleep in the morning, because I've already bathed and shaved, and you've already made breakfast."

I thought about it for a minute. "I don't know," I said. "Somehow I don't think *The Air Force Wife* would approve."

☆ ★ ☆ **4** ☆ ★ ☆

POLICE THOSE QUARTERS; LIFT THAT BALE

One would think, human nature being what it is, that my first few months as a housewife would have been spent scrubbing, cleaning, dusting, and rinsing out the vegetable bins.

The Air Force Wife certainly had this in mind. After all, it reminded me, I'd been given a golden opportunity, a chance to nurture and care for a government employee and his home. And if I wanted to qualify for periodic re-enlistment, I'd better live up to the task.

My approach to "home management," therefore, had better not be casual or haphazard. Organization was what was expected of me, and organized was what I'd be wise to get. I was allocated two hours daily. In that time I was to perform all household duties prescribed. From the sound of it the prescription had been issued by no less than a committee of lieutenant generals in the Pentagon. For as *The Air Force Wife* pointed out, if I chose to use any portion of these two hours for such frivolities as reading the paper or washing my hair, I should be prepared to deduct the time from later moments allotted for leisure.

The starting gun, as it were, was to be fired shortly after I'd sent "my hero" off to work. I was then to follow steps one through eight, and so progress through an orderly day till, when it came time for taps, I could retire with my head held high, my conscience clear, and my venetian blinds dust-free.

Unfortunately *The Air Force Wife*'s approach to housework and mine differed drastically. It never occurred to me, for instance, to buy a "special wastebasket on rollers for discarded flowers and ashes." But then I wasn't managing a funeral parlor either.

I resented the instruction "Tune in on a food program (on the radio) while drying the dishes. It will give you ideas in planning your meals." I preferred to tune in on *As the World Turns* so I could get ideas in planning my next bout with amnesia or brain surgery.

I balked at being told when to shop, how to serve lunch, and when to allow for "personal beautifying and mental improvement." What did they care about my mental improvement? They'd taken my morning paper away, telling me, "No, no, police your quarters first." And now that the news was old and I'd accidentally wrapped section B around the garbage, they wanted me to catch up on things.

But it was the directions for the dinner hour that really set my teeth on edge. "A weary husband," I was told, "may enjoy a cocktail before dinner."

"Good Lord," I snarled, "more of the masculine bill of rights. Does it ever end?"

". . . or it may be equally restful for him to have a quiet talk with you as an unhurried companion."

"Marvelous. And who's to get dinner while you two loll around chatting?"

"Sometimes he may like to listen to the radio, and make informative remarks on the news to you."

"Well, that follows. I wasn't allowed to read the news till I'd policed my quarters, and I had to listen to a 'rutabaga update' on the radio, so I haven't the faintest idea what's going on in the world."

"After dinner, never ask your husband to help with the dishes. He has been working for the government all day."

"Do you subscribe to all this drivel?" I asked Joe one night when he, the weary husband, was enjoying a cocktail, and I, the weary wife and hurried companion, was breaking protocol and having one of my own.

He paused, too long in my opinion, and a wistful look fluttered across his face.

"Well, do you?"

"Oh, no," he said. "That's pre–World War Two stuff. Don't let all those directives bother you. Just do things the way you always have."

Unfortunately the way I'd always done things was not particularly commendable. My only instinctive talent was that I made marvelous lists. They were a thing of beauty:

I. Clean bedroom.
  A. Bed.
    1. Remove sheets and pillow cases.
       a) Wash sheets and pillow cases.
       b) Dry.
       c) Fold and put away.
  B. Dresser.
    1. Dust.
    2. Arrange lipsticks.
       a) See if you can find the pink lipstick that goes with your blue dress.

I even left room at the end for additions—"Get dressed" or "Have breakfast"—then I'd cross them off with a flourish and feel as if I'd accomplished something.

Of course, as luck would have it, my enthusiasm waned once the list was complete, and because I'd elected to take Latin in high school instead of the full complement of Home Ec courses, my skills were spotty. I was missing the automatic impulses rumored to whisper into every woman's ear, "Don't just stand there, dear. Wipe off the top of the refrigerator."

Consequently, once I'd finished my list, I'd also come to the end of my proficiency. So from then on it was stream-of-consciousness cleaning.

"Let's see. I have to clean the bedroom and change the bed—but first I'd better pick up these papers and stack them—oh, wait a minute—there was a chicken and almond recipe I was going to cut out—I think it was in Wednesday's paper—yes, here it is—I'll get the scissors—I think they're in the kitchen drawer—oh, Lord, I forgot to soak the egg dishes—I better do that or I'll never get them clean—what's the matter with this faucet?—it's spraying all over—probably needs tightening—I'll get the wrench—here it is—oh, there are the scissors too—I might as well cut out that recipe while I have them . . ."

And so it went. By midmorning the apartment looked as if it had been stirred with a stick, and I still hadn't changed the bed. Had I any close friends in town, I would have called them up, suggested lunch out, then whirled through my chores like an efficiency expert run amuck, so I'd be able to go with a clear conscience.

But I was the new girl in town. I didn't have any close friends. I didn't even know anyone. There was Mrs. Mackie, of course, but she was rarely home. Our neighborhood was mostly geriatric; and like an old hunting dog stretched out in front of the fire it blinked occasionally and twitched its tail, but didn't rise to greet me.

The other Air Force wives, those I'd met at the wedding, were scattered in apartments of their own all over the city. Besides, with only a couple of months of P-RI school left, they were busy sorting through drawers, weeding out closets, and preparing to move on to their new assignments.

Our new assignment, which came through in late February, was to stay where we were, at Sheppard, with Joe teaching what he'd recently learned. So for the time being at least I teetered alone on my little raft of domesticity and tried haphazardly to keep the flotsam and the jetsam in their place.

My success was minimal. So half an hour before Joe was due, panic hit me, and I flew from room to room picking up, putting away, washing, rinsing, and tucking in at the edges. By the time I heard his car pull up and he walked in the door, there was a fair semblance of order, but only fair. It was nothing that would have passed inspection; and though my last waking thought each night was Tomorrow I'll really get organized, I rarely did.

I continued to putter, to dab, and to whisk. Occasional bursts of the nesting instinct had me scrubbing and polishing and ironing dish towels. But as time wore on, it became apparent that housework was not my forte, and I searched for legitimate ways to avoid it.

"Maybe if I got a job," I told Joe one night as I wandered around staring at my current sins of omission: the dust on the coffee table, the pile of books and magazines on top of the TV, the mottled kitchen floor, the combustible oven, the cobwebs in the corner behind the couch. "Maybe if I were working I wouldn't get so bored, and I'd do a better job in the time I had. You know what they say. The more you do, the more you can do."

Joe was paying bills at the time, and he looked up enthusiastically. "It's an idea," he said. "It's definitely an idea." Then he thought a minute and I could almost see him leap to the other side of the fence. "But then again I'm not saying you have to. I don't want you to feel that I've forced you." Another vault over the pickets. "Still we sure could use the money." He sighed and mumbled, "God knows how we could use the extra money."

That I knew. I'd had my first clue when Joe sold the brand-new powder-blue air-conditioned Chrysler he'd courted me in, and we went down to Happy Harry's Used Car Lot and picked up a 1952 Pontiac with one window that wouldn't open. Clues two through twelve followed in rapid succession, and soon it was apparent that marriage was expensive, and we were going to have to struggle to make ends meet.

Joe seemed surprised. Why I don't know. His Cousin Winnie had warned him, way back when he first showed her the engagement announcement in the paper. She'd taken one look at my statistics—which included a high school diploma from Annie Wright Seminary, a boarding school in Tacoma, a degree from that fancy Eastern college Smith, and an admission that, God forbid, I was an Episcopalian—and she'd thrown up her hands in horror.

"Oh, Joe Robert," she'd wailed, "this woman's nothing but a gold digger. I can tell. Why, she's going to run through your money as fast as she can."

True to her prediction, I did. It hadn't taken long. In fact I'd hardly been aware I was squandering his wealth on rent and groceries, depleting his checking account by buying soap rather than making it from lye and bacon grease, and insisting he pamper me with luxuries like "store bought" mayonnaise and an occasional bottle of bourbon. But aware or not, I'd done it; and though Cousin Winnie would have been equally appalled at the thought of my deserting my scrub bucket and sudsy ammonia in favor of the sin-soaked life of a working woman, I decided to give it a try.

Had I known the civilian attitude toward employment of military dependents, I wouldn't have bothered. For at the time it was easier to make it as a monotone in the Mormon Tabernacle Choir than it was to be an Air Force wife and be hired as a part-time cashier at a grocery store.

The excuse was "If I hire you and you're reassigned, then where will I be?" Actually the townspeople didn't cotton to us military types. Like Cousin Winnie, they knew our kind and they knew we were no good.

I, however, was blissfully unaware of this. So I went ahead with my plans. The place to start, I decided, was with the North Texas State Employment Agency. On the appointed morning I got up early. Why, I don't know. Nothing opened till nine, but I was nervous. What if I wore the wrong thing? What if I said something inane, or even something overly ane, for that matter? What if they asked me to take a typing test?

That was the trouble with being a liberal arts major. I could recite passages from *The Waste Land* and recognize the subjunctive case if pressured, but I couldn't type more than twenty-odd words a minute. As for dictation, I might as well be asked to take notes in Urdu.

Joe tried to allay my fears. "You'll do fine," he said just before he left for class. "In fact you'll bowl them over. Now don't worry."

But I did. So much so that for two hours I paced from room to room inadvertently wiping, straightening, and dusting. And by nine I'd not only bathed and dressed, I'd also cleaned the apartment till it shone.

Finally it was time to go. I wore the traditional Smith "job interview" costume: a suit, simple and conservative; a collarless blouse, tastefully accented by a single strand of pearls; gloves; a hat in an accent color; and plain pumps. Before I went out the door, I checked to be sure my seams were straight. Who knows, I thought, a crooked seam snaking its way up the side of my leg might easily cost me my job.

Little did I know. The North Texas State Employment Agency couldn't have been less concerned with whether or not my seams were straight.

I drove downtown, parked on a side street, and checked in the rearview mirror one more time to be sure I looked presentable. Then, having no more reason to delay, I got out of the car and headed off to seek my fortune.

If I expected opulence, with low lighting, carpeting, and fresh flowers on the receptionist's desk, I got over it immediately. The employment office was a large room bathed in linoleum and fluorescent light. The walls were institutional green, and over the several windows venetian blinds hung askew like kicked-out hems. To my left were desks with shirtsleeved men who sat at them and ruffled through the paperwork lethargically. To my right men in overalls slouched on rows of folding chairs. More were wedged together on a wooden deacon's bench against the wall. They looked as if they were waiting for the first chords of a piano recital.

When I walked in they turned to stare. Immediately I wished I'd left my hat at home. For even in my bargain-table suit and blouse, I felt like an officer of the Junior League on an inspection tour.

Apparently the receptionist noticed the resemblance too. Her "May I help you?" intimated I'd come in the wrong door.

"Yes," I said, "I've come to see about a job." I tried to work my gloves off nonchalantly and stuff them in my purse.

"Do you have an appointment?"

"No, I didn't think I needed one."

"Actually you don't. But as you can see we're pretty busy today. You can wait if you want, or," she added brightly, "if you have some shopping to do you can come back later."

I knew if I left I'd lose my nerve. "I'll wait," I said. Then I gave her my name, found a chair at the back, and sat down.

It was a long wait. One by one those handing out the jobs called the roll. "Billy Diamond?" "Elvin Shay?" "Chester Yoder?" One by one my fellow unemployed rose and shuffled over to a desk. They didn't seem eager. Nor did the interviewers. I could tell from the look on their faces they weren't expecting to find candidates for a career in advertising or banking. Bodies seemed to be what they needed: strong healthy bodies.

I wondered how I'd do on a road crew, or whether I'd be sent off to carry mortar and hods for a project out at the base.

Finally around noon my turn came. The room was almost empty. Clerks had gone off to lunch. The employable presumably had gone off to be employed. I was the only one left. For a while I thought they'd forgotten me. Then one of the men waved me over to his desk. His enthusiasm, what there was of it, had vanished sometime around eleven, and his energy seemed due to depart at any minute.

"Well now," he said, rummaging though one of the drawers in his desk, "what can I do for you?" He gestured for me to sit.

"I'm looking for a job."

He sighed, rubbed at his eyes, and took out a blank form. "I assumed that," he said. "All right. I'll need your name, your address, and your phone number."

I answered each of his questions, and he scribbled something in the appropriate box. "OK." He sighed again. "Have you finished high school?" The tone in his voice predicted a negative answer.

"Yes."

He brightened infinitesimally, but I could tell he wasn't about to get his hopes up. "Have you gone any farther?"

"Yes, I have a B.A. from Smith College."

His head snapped up. "You do?"

"Yes. I graduated last June. I was an English major."

He pushed his chair back and stood up. "Hey, Glenn," he called across the room, "come here quick. I want to show you something."

Glenn hurried over.

"Lookee here. This lady's got a college degree." They both examined the application form, and my new admirer turned to me. "My God," he said, "I can't tell you what this does for me. Why you're the first educated person we've had here in months." He thought a moment. "Say, what kind of job are you looking for?"

I was still recovering from his effusiveness. "I don't know," I said. "Just about anything. What I'd really like is a job that has to do with writing. But I'm sure you haven't any of those."

"Oh, I don't know." He grabbed the phone and dialed. "We'll see about that." He waited, listening. "Hello, Randy? Bill Reiter here, over at the employment office. Say, is Phil in?" He covered the phone with his hand. "I'm calling Phil Ollman, the editor at the *Times*. Hello, Phil? Bill Reiter. Say, Phil, I've got a lady here in my office who's a graduate of Smith College, and she needs a job. I thought you folks might have something." He paused. "Yeah . . . Smith." He turned to me. "That's in Missouri, isn't it?"

"No, Massachusetts. Stephens is in Missouri."

"Anyway, Phil, she's got a degree in English, and she writes. So I told her you might have a job for her." He laughed. "I bet she can write better than anyone you've got over there now."

I doubted that. So apparently did Phil.

"Well, yeah, she is," Bill Reiter said after listening for a time. "But her husband's been reassigned to Sheppard for a four-year tour." He waited. "OK . . . yeah . . . I understand. Well, let me know if you change your mind." He hung up.

"Sorry," he said. "Some people around here are funny about hiring military dependents. Frankly I think he's afraid you'll correct his grammar. God knows I wish somebody would. But don't worry. We'll find you a job—easy."

That night I gave Joe the whole story. "I can't get over it," I said. "He really sounded as if I'd have no trouble finding a job."

But it was not to be. Apparently Bill Reiter was the only person in town who cared whether or not I had a degree. It certainly made no impression on the folks at the Pampered Princess.

"Honey," Mrs. Nevitt, the owner, told me as she adjusted a wayward slip strap, "it's not that I wouldn't hire you in a minute. Lord knows we need someone. But what happens if your husband gets orders?"

Farley Brewster of Lucille's Decor felt the same way. So did the personnel manager at Lamar's Department Store.

So I gave up, for the time being at least. I could hear *The Air*

Force Wife cheering in the background. It had, after all, warned me that ". . . a wife should not work . . . simply to improve one's standard of living or to buy a piano . . . if such work in any way jeopardizes your home responsibilities."

☆ ★ ☆ **5** ☆ ★ ☆

GUESS WHO'S COMING TO WHAT AND WHEN?

Broadway producers are smart. They open out of town and test their wares on audiences in Philadelphia and New Haven before bringing the final show to New York.

I wasn't so lucky. The moment Joe learned he was being reassigned to Sheppard, he announced the time had come to start entertaining—at home—without so much as a rehearsal.

"What do you mean the time has come to start entertaining?" I shouted when he first brought the subject up.

"Just that. I think it would be a good idea to have some of the men I'm going to be working with and their wives over for dinner."

"But Joe," I wailed, "I still haven't mastered having you over for dinner. It's all I can do now to get a simple meal on the table at a reasonable hour with all the hot items still hot, all the cold items still cold, and the carrots somewhere this side of crunchy. And here you are suggesting I perform my feeble act for strangers."

"Oh, come now, it's not as bad as all that."

"It is. Believe me. Haven't you ever heard of the unwritten rule that a bride should never be asked to give a dinner party till she's practiced for at least six months?"

"You're making that up."

"No I'm not." I was, but I wasn't about to admit it. "Remember I told you about Sally's fiasco, when Jack invited hordes of relatives over for dinner the first month they were married, and she had a ten-pound roast, and misread the cookbook and only cooked it for twenty-nine minutes."

"That's different."

"No it isn't. That poor girl had to slice off hunks of bloody meat and take them into the kitchen and broil them. She was mortified."

Joe chuckled at the thought of it all, and I could see I'd have to come up with another example. "What about my friend Lee?" I said. "She had a dinner party before she was ready, and not till the guests had gone home did she realize that everything she'd served was white. Chicken, mashed potatoes, cauliflower, rolls. She even had vanilla ice cream."

"Oh, well. I'm sure no one noticed."

"Are you kidding? It was all over town in three days. She was so embarrassed she didn't leave the house for a week."

Joe put his arm around me. "Well you're not Lee," he said, "and you're not Sally. Besides," he added, avoiding my gaze, "I've already asked the Gibbs and the Eplers to come over a week from next Saturday."

"You what?"

"I asked the Gibbs and the Eplers to come over." He put his hand over my mouth, presumably to stifle the scream. "Now don't get upset. It will be fine. You don't have to have anything fancy. They know that you're new at this." His words were tumbling over each other. "And I'll help. I promise. I'll peel and scrub and mash, whatever you need. I'll even help clean the house." He paused and slowly took his hand away. "Really, honey," he said, "it'll be fun."

I stared at him for a minute, then sat down. "But Joe," I said, "I don't even know the Gibbs and Eplers. If you had to issue an invitation, why couldn't it have been to someone I know?"

"You know them. Remember you met them at the New Year's Eve party at the club."

"I met hundreds of people that night. Good Lord, we weren't even married, and I was so conscious of being 'So you're Joe's fiancée,' I could meet them all again, in order, and I wouldn't recognize a single name or face."

"Now, now, you're just upset. It'll be fine. I promise. Both Captain Gibb and Captain Epler are easygoing friendly guys, and I'm sure their wives are just as—"

"Captain?" I was on my feet again. "Captain?" I shrieked. "It's not enough you invite people for dinner without telling me. It's not enough they are perfect strangers, but now you tell me they're captains."

"What's so special about captains?" Joe had been in this man's Air Force for seven years. I was still new, and like an eighth-grader who thinks the sophomores are next to God, I was in awe of superior rank. I'd soon get over that, but for the time being, with all my domestic and military skills as yet unhoned, I felt inferior, unworthy, and terrified. Luckily Joe didn't bring up the old platitude about "They put their pants on one leg at a time." I might have hit him if he had.

"I don't know what's so special about captains," I moaned. "I only know the whole idea scares me."

"Well don't let it." I sensed he was tiring and the Air Force officer was about to come forward to dismiss the troops. "You have two weeks to get ready; and before you know it, it will be over and it will have been a great success."

Little did he know. Two weeks was plenty of time if all one had to do was climb a mountain, or walk across the state, but as far as I could see I needed at least twice that for everything I had to do.

As it turned out, a couple of months would have been more like it.

On the first Monday, the day I'd set aside for doing the laundry and getting that out of the way, the seven-year-old Texas drought broke. Had I had a washing machine and a dryer, it would have been no problem. I didn't. I washed our clothes by hand in the tub, and hung them on Mrs. Mackie's line.

The rain started half an hour after I'd put them all in to soak.

"Oh, well," I said to myself as I stared out the window and watched the drops kick up little puffs of dust as they hit the ground. "It should clear off by afternoon."

It didn't, and that night after dinner Joe helped me string up temporary clotheslines in the living room and dining room.

On Tuesday the rain continued.

By Wednesday puddles were lapping at the door. I put on my bathing suit, borrowed the Mackies' shovel, and dug trenches around the apartment.

It cleared briefly on Thursday, long enough for me to get the laundry, which was still damp and beginning to smell, out to the line. Not long enough, however, for it to dry. I ran out at the first clap of thunder, and twenty minutes later I had it draped all over the house again.

On Friday, for a reason I have yet to understand, Joe stopped by the pound on the way home and picked out a puppy.

"Surprise," he said as he came in the door with a large box and a bag of food in his hand. "I brought you an early birthday present."

"But Joe—"

"Remember last week when you said someday you wanted us to get a dog?"

"But—"

"That someday is here. Besides, I thought you could use some cheering up."

Cheer me up? It was only sheer will power that was keeping me from slashing at my wrists with a rusty nail.

"What about Felicia?" I bleated weakly.

"What about her? They'll get along fine. He's just a puppy, and you know cats don't take out after puppies." He put the box down. "Here, I'll show you. I'll go get her. Where is she?"

"I don't know. I haven't seen her all day."

"Then I'll find her." He pranced off into the other room.

I stared down at the box and the shivering little ball of brown fur. "I guess I did say I wanted a dog someday," I muttered, patting

47

him gently, trying to reassure him. "But as I remember, I also said I'd like an emerald ring, and my own car."

"Hey Annie," Joe yelled from the bedroom, "come here. Look at what I found."

I didn't like the tone of his voice. It suggested he'd found something more exciting than a new puppy, and I was already up to my gunwales in excitement.

I was right. He'd located Felicia, in the corner of our closet. She, who had seemed circumspect and always ladylike despite the numerous suitors who'd howled outside our door, was giving birth to a litter of kittens.

I left the room, went back to the dog, and burst into tears.

Saturday and Sunday were spent tending the new mother, bathing the dog, who was host to an entire civilization of fleas, and keeping them apart. The dog—tentatively christened Vicar in honor of Daddy and all men named Vincent who had little or no chance of having grandchildren named after them—felt insecure. He whined and yipped and missed the papers I'd spread through the apartment.

Felicia tended her family of five, hissed at Vicar, and yowled to go out and tell the world she was a mother. Joe flitted between the two and marveled at the wonders of birth, puppyhood, and having seven pets.

I contemplated drink and wondered, What next?

On Tuesday I found out. The bathroom sink clogged. I attacked it with the traditional unbent coat hanger. It pierced through the ancient pipe and flooded the bathroom floor.

"Dammit to hell, Joe," I said as we slapped towels down on the floor, dragged them up again, and tried to wring them out in the tub. "How can we expect to have a dinner party with five kittens mewing in the closet, a puppy traipsing from room to room like a leaky bucket, and a hole in the bathroom pipe?"

"Now, now, honey, don't worry." He pushed a towel under the tub and hauled it back out again. "Believe me, everything is going to be fine."

So said he. Everything was not going to be fine. I was certain of it; it wouldn't have surprised me at all if at that precise moment the ceiling had collapsed.

It didn't, however, so we cleaned up the bathroom; and the floor, already corrugated, warped further. Then Joe contacted Mr. Mackie, who fixed the pipe. Now it was time to give my full concentration to the dinner ahead.

Mother, in response to a desperate postcard pleading for one of her never-fail-when-company's-coming menu suggestions, had air-mailed me her recipe for shrimp curry with condiments. Thoughtfully she included detailed instructions.

"Cardamom may be skipped if you don't have any handy." I didn't. I'd barely had time to accumulate salt, pepper, and cinnamon.

"Powdered ginger may be substituted for green ginger root or chopped preserved ginger. It'll be in the spice section of your store in a red and white can."

She knew me well, and knew I needed directions.

"Don't cut your bananas or chop your eggs till you're ready to serve, as they'll turn brown."

I read it over and over till I had it memorized. Then, like an engine that finally catches hold, I leapt forward rinsing, dusting, polishing, sweeping, mopping, washing, mincing, chopping, peeling, and generally doing in three days what most people accomplish in a few hours.

At last Saturday evening arrived. Felicia and company were spending the evening in a box out in the Mackies' garage. Vicar, with his attendant roomful of newspapers, was safely ensconced in our bedroom, where, Joe assured me, there wasn't a chance in a million he'd be able to climb up on the bed.

With half an hour to go, dinner preparations were at a fever pitch. Pots simmered and gurgled on the back of the stove. The condiments trembled in their separate bowls waiting for the moment of presentation. And the silver and crystal glittered on the table.

While I changed my earrings for the third time, and considered changing my dress as well, Joe occupied himself in the living room with ice and mixers and bowls of nuts.

At seven sharp, the precise time mentioned in the invitation, they all arrived. It's an old military tradition under the subheading of "Promptness is the essence of good leadership." I was grateful. Had they been late I would have had more time to see the dust ball lurking under the couch. I would have had a chance to ponder whether or not we'd run out of ice, and to worry that Vicar might escape and disgrace us all.

Joe answered the door and ushered them single file through the kitchen and into the dining room.

"Annie," he said, "you remember Nick and Connie Gibb. They were at the next table at the club on New Year's Eve."

"Of course," I lied, extending my hand to the tall dramatic pair he'd indicated. "How nice to see you again."

"And these are the Eplers, Rob and Jan."

"Hello."

Rob shook my hand. "We weren't there that night," he said. "Jan had an allergy attack, and she didn't think her red eyes matched her dress." He laughed, and Jan as if to verify his statement sneezed.

"Oh, that's too bad," I said, and then because I must have a death wish I added, "Are you allergic to a lot of things?"

"No, no"—she fumbled in her purse for a handkerchief—"just dust and animal fur."

"Well," Joe broke in as a sinking feeling hit the pit of my stomach, "let me take your coats, and we'll all go into the living room."

I rushed to intercept. "Here, honey," I said, "let me have them. I'll put them on our bed."

"Oh, all right." He handed them over. "Now let's see," he said. "What can I get anyone to drink? I've got scotch, gin, bourbon, and an assortment of mixers."

"No tequila?" Rob asked, slapping him on the back. "Hell Joe, you know Nick's favorite drink is tequila sunrise."

They all chortled at a private joke, and I waited till they'd shuffled past. Then I opened the bedroom door a crack and slithered in before Vicar could squeeze past me.

"Now you hush," I said as he attacked my ankles. I put the coats in the exact center of the bed where he couldn't reach them, then slipped out and closed the door tightly behind me.

Conversation bubbled in the living room, but before I joined everyone, I dashed into the kitchen to get some hot hors d'oeuvres I had in the oven. Then I took a deep breath and made my entrance.

"Well, that takes care of that," I trilled, being at a loss for a more scintillating remark. "Now who would like a cheese puff? Mrs. Gibb?"

Connie Gibb swiveled around in her chair. "Ann, honey chile," she said, "for heaven's sake call me Connie." Her accent was an odd mixture of Hermione Gingold and Minnie Pearl, and I tried to reconcile this with the fact Joe had told me she was from California. "The last time someone called me Mrs. Gibb," she continued, "was when I had to go see Donnie's teacher." She tossed her head back and slapped the arm of the chair; and four bracelets, an Indian toe ring, and what must have been fifteen years' worth of silver charms jangled and clanked together like a herd of tambourines. "Remember that Nick?" she said. "Donnie stuffed paper towels into the toilet at nursery school and caused a minor flood, so we had to go in for a conference and promise he'd never do it again." She exploded with another laugh, and her earrings—a string of graduated temple bells—joined in the merriment.

"I remember," Nick muttered, juggling a handful of peanuts. He tossed one into the air and caught it in his mouth. "I remember all right."

He seemed ill at ease, standing over by the door and shifting from one foot to the other. I gathered he didn't find Donnie's antics quite so hilarious. He threw another peanut in the air and it clanked against his teeth as he caught it.

"Say Joe," he said changing the subject, "did I show you the new trick I learned the other day?" He put his drink down and reached into his pocket. He brought out a pack of cards. "It's a great one."

There was a sigh from the couch. I looked over just in time to see Rob give Jan a poke. She ignored him, pasted on a bright smile, and absent-mindedly scratched her knee, where I could see a welt forming. Rob jabbed her again.

"Joe's seen all your tricks, Nick," he said affably. "We all have. We've seen your disappearing quarter trick, your match in the ear trick, and your wandering ace of spades trick. Why don't you have another drink instead?"

I watched as Nick's already long and baleful face fell further.

"I haven't," I found myself saying. Why, I don't know. I hate

51

card tricks. I hate any tricks. The mere sound of "Pick a card, any card," makes me hyperventilate. But what could I do. He looked so sad.

Right away I knew I'd made a mistake. He bounded to my side, and for the next half hour while everyone else laughed and talked and told the one about the foreign minister's hunting dog, I was a prisoner of aces that rose to the top of the deck and queens that hid in coat pockets.

Finally when I could say, "Oh, my, how'd you do that?" no longer, Joe rescued me.

"Isn't dinner about ready?" he asked during a brief shuffling break.

"Oh, it is. It is," I said too eagerly. "Give me a minute to put everything on the table." I fled into the kitchen before the trap could snap shut again. Minutes later I called them in.

Dinner went smoothly. Joe, ever the genial host, saw to it that the wine flowed along with the conversation. I did notice that Jan was less excited with the prospect of peanuts, chutney, bananas, and eggs on her curry. And when Joe urged her to have another sardine, it seemed she recoiled slightly. But when she regained her composure and insisted she was full, I gave her the benefit of the doubt.

The rest ate heartily and I relaxed. I shouldn't have. For Nick, his magic show completed, with little hope of requests for an encore, was lying in wait. I might have sensed he was up to something when he cleared his throat several times and kept glancing around the room as if on an inspection tour. But I was too relieved to have made it this far without a pipe bursting or Vicar revealing that he and his animal fur were on the other side of the bedroom door. And I was too busy telling myself, By God, Ann, you've done it. You've given a dinner party, to recognize the obvious signs.

So when there was a brief lull and Nick jumped in with "Say, do you folks have a vacuum cleaner?" I was completely surprised.

"A vacuum?" I said. "Why no, we don't. Does it show that much?"

"Oh, no. I just wondered, that's all." He was silent and we all waited.

Finally Connie broke the silence. "Oh, come on, Nick," she said. "Don't be so mysterious. Tell them." She gestured and her bracelets rattled against her wine glass. "Nick sells vacuum cleaners," she announced.

I don't know why I was surprised. Somehow it was fitting that an amateur magician should also be a vacuum cleaner salesman. But perhaps I still labored under the delusion that Air Force captains were above going door to door with a satchelful of brushes and disposable bags. Apparently I was alone.

"Oh, Nick," Rob groaned, "you're not going to try and sell another one of those lousy vacuum cleaners, are you?"

"What do you mean lousy? You like yours, don't you?"

"Well sure, but—"

"Oh, Rob," Jan broke in, "you know we do. Why only this morning I used ours to defrost the refrigerator, and heaven knows, I'd never be able to keep up with this Texas dust if we didn't have our vacuum."

That was all Nick needed. He pushed his chair back, excused himself momentarily, and loped out to his car to haul in a demonstration model.

Then for an hour or more he switched nozzles and heads, produced extension wands, and showed us how to clean the grillwork on the back of the refrigerator. Finally we succumbed.

After that the evening ended. It had to. We'd been about as hospitable as we could. Besides it was late.

I went in to get the coats while Joe listened to the final words on the venetian blind attachment. Vicar had clawed his way up the bedspread, and was happily asleep on Nick's coat. I dusted it off, and made sure Jan's gray raincoat was free of animal fur. Not till later did I notice Vicar had chewed off one of Nick's buttons too.

"Do you think he'll notice?" I asked Joe as we were cleaning up.

"Hell no," he said. "But if he does, I'll tell him it's simply the old disappearing button trick."

☆ ★ ☆ 6 ☆ ★ ☆

THEY'RE CHANGING GUARDS AT BUCKINGHAM PALACE

Spring never comes to Wichita Falls. Winter does. Lord knows summer certainly does. But in between it's like a tennis match with the wind whistling a snowstorm by your ear one day, then lobbing a heat wave over your head the next.

I never got used to it. Spring is supposed to be tulips and daffodils, not frostbite and sunburn. Consequently I cursed the weather daily as I rummaged through my drawers for either a pair of shorts and a sleeveless blouse, or an overcoat and mittens.

"You'd think it would make up its mind," I muttered to myself one day in early March. I was at the clothesline being systematically whipped to death by wet socks and pillow cases. "You'd think the wind would quiet down for a while and give spring a chance to wander in."

"Whatcha want to wander in?" a voice behind me broke into my monologue.

I jumped and turned around. It was little Jimmie Mackie. He

and his dachshund puppy, an inseparable pair, had come out of their house without my hearing them and were now working on an excavation project in the yard.

I think the puppy's name was Mert. But Jimmie never called her Mert. She was "mah—dawg—mah—little—hawt—dawg." Jimmie, like his mother, spoke in a languid drawl. He surrounded each word with his mouth, swirled it around for a while, then, when he was good and ready, let it roll out. Sometimes I had trouble remembering what it was he'd started to say.

"Are you talking to me?" I asked as I unwrapped a bath towel the wind had twirled around my arm.

"Yup." He scooped out a shovelful of dirt and Hawt Dawg stuck her nose into the hole to see how much farther they had to go. "Ah said whatcha want to wander in?"

"To wander in? Oh, I was just wishing spring would wander in."

"It's gonna," he said.

"Yeah, but when?"

"When we move."

"What do you mean 'When we move'?"

He dragged Hawt Dawg out of the hole and scraped out some more dirt. "Momma says it's gonna be spring when we move."

"You're moving?"

"Sure. Didn't I just tell you we were?" He shook his head impatiently. Then because the puppy had wandered off and was trying to squeeze through the slats in the fence, he bounded after it.

"Did you know the Mackies were moving?" I asked Joe that night when he came home.

"Oh, I forgot to mention it. Yes, Mr. Mackie told me about it yesterday."

"Where are they going?"

"They're moving to a farm out in the country."

"But what about this place?"

"As I understand it, the people who own the farm, I think their name is Ohrbeck, are trading places with them. They're moving here, and the Mackies are going there."

"Why?"

"I don't know for sure. Mr. Mackie says it's because they can't afford to board that pony she won. But I think he's a farm boy at heart, and just wants a place outside the city."

"Oh. . . . Did he say anything about what the other people were like? The—the— What was their name?"

"The Ohrbecks. No, I haven't the faintest idea. All I know is they have two small boys, and I think the grandfather and an old aunt live with them."

"Does that mean we're going to have to move—to make room for the grandfather and the aunt?"

"No, no. Mr. Mackie said he'd told the Ohrbecks that we'd asked to live here till base housing became available, and they agreed."

"Well that's a relief." I went into the kitchen to start dinner. "Say," I yelled in to him, "did he say when all this was going to take place?"

"I'm not sure, but I gather it'll be in the next week or two."

Joe was right. On Friday the Mackies started hauling in cardboard boxes. All weekend long they worked sorting through this, throwing out that. Jimmie and Hawt Dawg didn't help matters. As fast as something was thrown out, they retrieved it.

"Ah got a wagon here," Jimmie told me on Sunday afternoon when I was headed out to the garbage, "and ah'm gonna fix it up, paint it, and sell it for a hunnert dollars."

Joe offered to help load the truck Mr. Mackie had borrowed from his brother-in-law, but they said they were sure they could manage it.

On Wednesday morning the moving van came. It didn't take them long to cart out what was left. Everything but the furniture and major appliances had already been transferred. By noon they were finished. I rushed over, afraid they'd go before I could say goodbye. Mrs. Mackie was in the kitchen sweeping up the last of the dust under the refrigerator.

"Gee I hate to see you leave," I said as I held the dust pan for her. "You all are about the only people we know around here."

She put the broom away. "Now don't you go and fret," she said. "We're expecting you and Joe to come out to the farm and visit with us. It's not that far, you know."

"I know," I said, "and we sure will."

We then traded regrets because we hadn't known each other longer. I thanked her for letting us keep Vicar, though early on he'd developed an abhorrence for Hawt Dawg and a passion for barking at odd hours. I offered her a place in my will for having found homes for Felicia's kittens. She sent her regards to Mother, who, inspired by Mrs. Mackie's successes, had enrolled herself in the Gwinett School of Contests, and was now on Lesson II: "Learning to Express Yourself in 25 Words or Less." Then after the traditional Southern benediction, "Y'all come see us now, heah?" she left.

Somehow I felt like an orphan. I'd been deserted. My security blanket had folded itself up and moved on. "I'm lonely," I told Joe when he came home.

"Lonely?"

"Yes. I miss the Mackies, and Jimmie, and Hawt Dawg."

"Oh, come now." He rolled his eyes back in his head. "You've got me, and Vicar, and Felicia. How can you be lonely?"

"I don't know. I just am. Besides, what if the Ohrbecks are horrible?"

"Oh, don't worry," he said. "I'm sure they'll be just as nice as the Mackies were."

Joe said that sort of thing a lot. It was his standard placebo statement designed to keep me from ranting on and on. It rolled out of his mouth automatically whenever my voice hit a certain pitch. He didn't even have to think about it.

"I don't think I'll ever find a job," I'd wail.

"Don't worry. I'm sure you will."

"I don't see how I can possibly lose enough weight to get into my blue dress by Saturday."

"Don't worry. I'm sure you can."

Every now and then I tried to cure him by slipping in a "Do you think I'll ever look as hideous as I did yesterday?"

He was too quick for me. "You didn't look hideous"—he'd sigh—"and I am too listening."

I certainly hoped he was right this time though. Our apartment was too close to the main house to be at odds with the landlord.

Luckily I didn't have long to wait. The next morning when I was hauling our collapsed mattress back onto its teetering slats so

I could try one more time to make the bed, I heard a truck drive up. I let the mattress flop back to the floor and went to see what was going on.

The whole family hadn't come. Only Mr. Ohrbeck and two young men he introduced as his brother's boys. They'd opened up the big wooden gate and driven a battered old truck up to the back door.

He was a small man, not much taller than I. He wore what looked like an old khaki uniform, a plaid workman's jacket, and a hat. He must have had several sets of this particular costume, for in the three months we lived there I never saw him wearing anything else. The hat, I suspected, had been on at birth, for inside, outside, no matter what the weather, it never left his head. At times I was tempted to ask him how he kept it on when the wind was whipping in off the plains, shredding flags on their poles, and waving branches around like frenzied spectators at a football game. But I never got up the nerve.

"Is there anything I can do to help?" I asked.

"Nope," he said, "nothin' right now." He stared at the ground, obviously ill at ease. "This is heavy work. Maybe later though when Momma and the kids come."

"All right."

He glanced up for a fleeting second. "Thanks anyway."

"No trouble."

I let myself into the apartment, making sure Vicar didn't escape and head off through the gate and down the street, and returned to the task of rebuilding our bed.

"Momma and the kids" didn't accompany him on his second trip or his third, and by late afternoon when Joe came home they still hadn't appeared.

"Maybe they're not coming till morning," I told Joe.

"Maybe not." He'd talked briefly to Mr. Ohrbeck, but as usual had failed to grill him for the information I wanted to hear.

Finally, shortly after dark, when I was up to my elbows in Brillo pads and dishwater, I heard a car drive up and doors slam.

"Junior? Elwood?" a high voice, perched on the edge of tolerance, split the air. "You boys stay away from there. You hear me? That's not our place."

She was too late. Our back door flew open, and there stood two little boys. The older one, about eight, was round. His head, with wispy blond hair, was round. His arms were round. His chubby hands were round, and his stomach, visible in the gap between the bottom of his T-shirt and the top of his jeans, was round.

"Hi," he said. "Who are you?"

"Ann. Who are you?"

"Junior. I'm Junior Ohrbeck—and this is Elwood." He reached around behind him and hauled his little brother forward. "Say hello, Elwood."

Elwood shook his head. He was about two. He had on red rubber boots, a diaper that was losing its battle with gravity, and an undershirt that flared at the bottom. His thumb was wedged in his mouth, and he clutched at the corner of a blanket that dragged behind him halfway across the yard. He stared up at me.

"Hello Elwood," I said as he inched back to safety behind Junior.

"You live here?" Junior asked, coming on in and giving the place a careful once-over.

"Yep."

"Me and Elwood's gonna live over there." He pointed to the other house. "Say," he said suddenly, "where's your mister?" By now Elwood had come in too, but his blanket had a way to go, so I held the door open for it.

"You mean Joe? Oh, he's in the living room."

"Good." He took that as an invitation and went to find him. Elwood and his blanket followed close behind. I could hear the surprise in Joe's voice when they announced their arrival. Then I gathered from the sound of the giggling that Vicar was also welcoming them to the neighborhood. I rinsed out the last of my pans and put it in the drainer.

"Elwood? Junior?" Their mother's voice searched the night again, and I went to tell her where they were. Apparently she'd already guessed. She was coming toward me when I got to the door.

"I'm sorry," she said when I confirmed her suspicions and held the door open so she too could come in. "I told them boys this place was yours. I told them to stay out. But you know how kids are, nosy, nosy, nosy." She sighed and ran her fingers through her

59

hair. Then she stopped. "Oh, my me, where are my manners." She laughed. "I'm Lettie, Lettie Ohrbeck. Looks like I'm your new landlady." She smoothed her print house dress over her plump sofa-pillow body and tugged at an old cardigan sweater.

"Hi, I'm Ann."

"Good to meet you. Now, where are those boys? Junior? Elwood?" she called. "You better get in here right now, or I'm going to slap you one upside the head."

They trotted back into the kitchen, and an amazed Joe and delirious Vicar followed close behind.

"Look, Momma," Junior said. "Joe here's got him a dog. Can we get a dog? Can we, can we, huh?"

"Lordy no, child." She grabbed him by the arm and headed him out the door. Then she picked up Elwood and his eternal blanket and plunked him on her hip. "We've got enough trouble with that cat of ours. Lord knows what we'd do with a dog." She turned to us. "We've got a cat. Call him Badger. Damn fool thing weighs well near to thirty pounds. I just hope he don't try running back to the farm. You know cats don't move places as good as dogs, and this one's pretty set in his ways." She sighed. "Oh, well, we'll see." She gave Junior, who was edging his way back in, a shove. "I gotta let you folks go," she said. "Lord knows I got enough work to do before we can get to bed tonight. Guess I'd better get on it. Oh, by the way," she said as she left, "Walt's dad—Grandpa O, we call him. Well, he's a little fuzzy up here"—she tapped her head—"and though we've told him this is your place, and he's to stay out, he gets muddled easy. So if he walks in, just turn him around and tell him, 'Wrong place, Grandpa O.' He'll go quiet.

"You don't have to worry about Aunt Mulie though. She never leaves the house." She chuckled. "She better not. Hasn't been out of her bathrobe in two years. You'll meet her. She's crazier than a bedbug. Keeps answering the door and talking to people who ain't there. But at least she's harmless." Lettie shrugged. "Don't know how I get stuck with all these looney relatives. You'd think Walt's brother would take 'em for a while." She stared into space. "Well," she said, shaking herself, "I can't stand here bending your ears all night. I got work to do. See ya." And she was gone.

I closed the door as she bellowed one final "Junior? Elwood? You come here this minute—you heah?"

"I kind of like her, don't you?" I said to Joe, who was still in shock.

"Yeah, I guess so."

"But do you think that the old man, you know, Grandpa O, is really going to be walking in here all the time?"

"Don't worry," Joe said. "I'm sure he won't."

Luckily Joe called it correctly. Grandpa O didn't come in. Instead he paced around the perimeter of the yard with a red coffee can clutched in his hand. This, Lettie explained, was " 'cause he chews tobacco and I won't let him spit on the ground."

Junior, however, was another story entirely. He bounded in like a firecracker, slamming the screen door behind him. Then he searched us out and said, "Hi, whatcha doin'?"

The answers varied, for Junior never knocked. When he did, he never bothered to wait for a "Come in."

"We're eating breakfast, Junior."

"I'm cleaning the tub out, Junior."

"Never you mind, Junior."

A single answer never satisfied him.

"How come you brush your teeth round and round, 'stead of up and down like Momma says?"

"Because I like to."

"You got toothpaste on your chin."

"I know."

"Grandpa O doesn't brush his teeth."

"Oh?"

"No. He takes them out and sticks 'em in a glass."

"That's because he has false teeth, teeth the dentist made for him."

"You got false teeth?"

"No."

"How 'bout Joe? Does he got false teeth?"

"No."

"When you gonna have a baby?"

"I don't know."

"How come?"

61

"Because."

And so it went till either Lettie screeched for him to come home, or I told him I thought I'd heard her screeching for him.

Elwood stayed home. He preferred to be with Lettie. Even when I went over to have coffee with her, he remained welded in her lap. Either that or he hid behind her chair with his blanket the only clue he was around.

When she baked he sat up on the big old kitchen table while she pounded and pummeled and sent up clouds of flour like Indian smoke signals.

"Elwood," she'd roar, swinging him down to the floor, "how many times do I have to tell you. Stay down." But he always scrambled back up. He knew she was all bluster.

I knew it too. For even though she complained constantly about the gaggle of relatives forced on her in one way or another, she always had a contingent over for Sunday dinner.

I'd hear about it on Monday.

"Girl," she'd say, pouring me a cup of rich, hot coffee, "I told Louise. She's my sister. She's the one who goes to the church where they talk in tongues and roll around in the aisle when the spirit moves them. I said to her, 'Louise, I'm sick and tired of being the one to cook dinner on Sundays. One of these days I'm going to up and refuse. Then where's everyone going to be?' " She would pause for a minute to let that soak in. Then she'd shake her head. "Poor old Louise, though," she'd say, "she can't do nothing'. Hell, since Barney up and left her and the kids she's lucky to be gettin food on the table at all."

"Isn't that the truth?" I'd cluck, nodding my head or shaking it, whichever seemed the most appropriate at the time. "Isn't that just the truth?"

I was over at Lettie's a lot. It was nice to have the company. Besides, if she wasn't calling me up to tell me she'd just fried up a batch of doughnuts, she was insisting I come over to do my laundry in her machine.

"No use you stomping around in that little bitty tub of yours," she'd say, "not with a perfectly good machine here."

So I'd gather up Joe's uniforms and whatever else was lolling in the hamper, and I'd trundle over to spend an hour or two listening to Lettie tell me what injustice had been forced on her now, while our clothes sloshed and jumbled in the washer.

After a while Elwood got used to me. So while his mother and I talked he'd crawl down off the table and try to get Badger to play horsie for him.

Lettie had not exaggerated when she described Badger. The cat was huge, as big as a good-sized dog. He had a purr that rattled windows and could be heard half a block away, and when he meowed it sounded like a squalling baby in mid-tantrum. Unfortunately he also fancied Felicia. The feeling was not reciprocated. So on hot nights, while Joe and I read or watched TV, he lurked on the other side of our screen door purring with feline passion, begging her to respond, and she hid under the couch and hissed. During the day, though, his main object in life was to avoid Elwood.

I rarely saw Aunt Mulie. She was like a wisp of smoke. She shimmered in the doorway, then vanished when I turned to say hello. I thought this was her pattern with everyone. Apparently not. Lettie said she told them I was evil. She'd seen me in a pair of shorts and a sleeveless blouse one day, and forever after she flitted from room to room with her gray hair standing on end and her bathrobe flapping out behind her, mumbling about "the evil nude lady."

"Ain't that a kick though," Lettie said one day when I was helping her with some ironing. "The old bat thinks you're a stripper here to lure Walt and Grandpa O down the road to hell."

I could just see Grandpa O standing at the gates of hell with his coffee can in his hand, and Walt, hat and all, beside him. "That's a kick all right," I said.

We had a good time, Lettie and I, and in a way I dreaded moving out to the base. Still I knew the day would come eventually when our name would rise to the top of the housing list and we'd have to go. Late in May it did.

It was hot that day, in the nineties as I remember. The air was still for once. Clothes dried on the line before they'd all been hung, and perspiration trickled down the hollow of my back.

"We picked a great day to iron," I said, fanning myself with a pair of Junior's shorts.

"Sure did." Lettie laughed. "But I'll warn you. It won't get any better. Leastwise not till October." She took a shirt out of the basket and sprinkled the collar. "Why don't you quit for a while?" she said. "You been helping me all morning, and we only got a couple of things left to iron."

"No, that's all right. I'm OK." I reached down to get a pillow case, and waited for her to finish with the sprinkling bottle.

"Hey, Ann." Junior burst in the back door. "Joe wants you. He's on the phone."

Lettie grabbed Junior's arm. "What do you mean he's on the phone? Did you go in their place again?" She cuffed him. "I'm going to smack you silly, boy, if you don't stay out of other people's places."

"But the phone was ringing," he protested. "All I did was go in to answer it."

"That's OK, Lettie," I said, unplugging my iron. "I'll be right back."

I ran across the yard and into our living room.

"Hello, Joe?"

"Where were you?"

"Just over at Lettie's."

"How come Junior was in the house?"

"He wasn't. He simply heard the phone and answered it. That's all. Now what did you want?"

"Well"—he paused for effect—"I've got news."

"What news?"

"I got a call from the housing office today."

"And . . . ?"

"And they have a place for us, on base, a two-bedroom place."

"They do?"

"Yep, and we can move in next week."

"Next week? Really?"

"That's what they said. How about that?"

"It's great . . . but."

"But what?"

"Oh, nothing. I was just thinking I'm going to miss Lettie, that's all. Then too this has been our first home together and it'll be sad leaving it."

"All right now. Don't go sentimental on me. Just think of it this way. We'll have two bedrooms, a real yard, a big kitchen, even a tub and shower. Also I'll only be five minutes away from work."

"You're right."

"Of course I am." He was all business, mainly because he knew that if he let himself go he could be more maudlin than I. He cleared his throat. "I've got to go now," he said. "I'll tell you more about it when I get home."

"It's a deal." I hung up. Imagine, I thought, a regular-sized tub and shower, plus a kitchen two people could move around in without first filing a flight plan. My mind raced ahead. I'd be able to go to the commissary myself. I wouldn't have to rely on Joe to do it. We'd have our own bed, one that stayed together. Maybe we could even buy a washing machine, and I could wash whenever the mood hit me.

I ran across the yard and bounded into Lettie's kitchen. "Guess what?" I said. "We've been given quarters on base."

She was hanging up a shirt. "You have?"

"Yes, Joe just got the word this afternoon."

"Why that's great." She seemed sincere. "Is it a nice place?"

"I don't know. I've never been in any of the duplexes on base, but Joe says it has two bedrooms, and I do know they all have tubs and showers."

"Boy, that'll be a change from that little wash basin you two got now."

"Won't it though." I stopped. "I am going to miss you though. I won't have anyone to talk to, and I'm sure no one out there makes fried doughnuts like you do."

She waved away my objections. "Don't be silly, girl," she said. "You'll make lots of friends out there. Besides, it's not like you're leaving the state. You'll be right across town. We'll see each other."

"Yeah," Junior added, his eyes bulging with excitement. "We'll come visit you, and Joe can take us out to see the planes, and . . . and . . ."

Suddenly Aunt Mulie floated into the room. She had an odd grin on her face, and she circled slowly, then whispered something to Lettie, and left.

"What was that?" I asked.

Lettie laughed. "Nothing much," she said. "She just heard you say you were moving, and she told me, 'Tell the nude lady goodbye.' "

I chuckled. "Goodbye, Aunt Mulie," I called. "Goodbye and good luck."

By the following Friday we were all packed up and ready to go.

"Take care of yourself," I said to Lettie as Joe paid her the last of the rent and gave her the key. "And don't you worry. We're coming back to see you—lots."

She yanked Junior away from the car and hiked Elwood up to a more comfortable position on her hip. "I'm counting on it," she said. "Now you two get out of here before I blubber."

As we drove down the street, I turned to look back. Aunt Mulie was on the front porch again, chattering at an invisible caller. Lettie and the children still stood waving. And Grandpa O circled back behind the clothesline on his morning rounds.

"Do you really think we'll come back a lot?" I asked Joe as he swung onto the main road.

"Don't worry," he said. "Of course we will."

☆ ★ ☆ 7 ☆ ★ ☆

FRIED NASTURTIUMS
OUT IN FRONT

Houses on an Air Force base are like the uniforms we used to wear
in boarding school. They have no glamour and little charm. But
since yours looks like mine, and ours looks like theirs, who cares?

Sheppard was no exception. The units were like offspring of the
buildings on base, all made of wood, all single-storied, and all painted
either milky yellow or gray. Each had a front porch, a back stoop,
and a brick planter for decoration. Unfortunately no plants ever
grew in the planters. Mainly because they all faced west, so in the
summer, even if you hosed the bricks down, they got so hot they
fried whatever vegetation had managed to struggle up and venture
into leaf. Still they remained, and each new family took a turn at
trying to coax a row of petunias or nasturtiums into feeble bloom.

Out in back were clotheslines, one to a family. And every now
and then a row of carports with an attendant storage area for the
inevitable woven lawn chairs and barbecues.

The majority of the units were two-bedroom affairs linked with another of their ilk to form a duplex. The floor plans were all the same. The front door opened directly into the living room. To the right, or to the left depending which side of the duplex was yours, was the kitchen. Straight ahead was a doorway into the hall, with a bathroom at one end, a bedroom at the other, and two doors in between. One of the two led to the second bedroom. The other was a closet. That was that. There were no foyers, no crannies, no bay windows, no sunken living rooms.

If you were lucky enough to be assigned quarters with three bedrooms, you got a variety of floor plans, even a frivolous nook or two. You also got SUD (single-unit dwellings), which meant you could yell obscenities at your husband without the neighbor's children repeating your words the next day.

We, however, didn't qualify for a three-bedroom unit. To do so we would have had to have several children, know the housing officer, have a date of rank in Gemini with Mercury on the cusp, and be anything but a lieutenant.

Our quarters were on Nehls Boulevard; 315B was the address. Of course, once we'd informed all our correspondents of the number and had ordered cases of personalized stationery and hundreds of return address labels, they changed it to 19B. This, I think, is an old Air Force custom born out of the need to think up new ways to keep all personnel busy at all times.

Nehls was the main street in the housing area. It ran from the guardhouse out on the Burkburnett Highway to the base itself. It also served as the demilitarized zone between the officers' housing and the enlisted men's housing. I never quite understood the need for this segregation. After all, they let airmen over the line so they could come fix our water heaters and check the pilot lights on our stoves. Why not mix up the housing? But it was not to be, and if you stood at one end of Nehls and looked down the street you could almost imagine a Civil War battlefield with ordered rows of troops advancing on each other, creeping forward till they were close enough to fire their muskets.

We were on the front line, so to speak—close enough for me to see the whites of their eyes, and to note in passing that their brick planters, facing east, abounded in nasturtiums and marigolds. Apparently a master sergeant had been lurking in the hall when Pentagon planners drew up their original grid.

We were in the area usually assigned to students. Sheppard Air Force Base was one of the four main technical training centers, and every nine months or so a new crop of men and their families pulled into town, unloaded their furniture, put their children in school, and settled down for a brief stay. Before you knew it they were gone, and a new family was moving in.

At times this was a blessing. When little Peter Granly, six, skinny, and louder than most air raid sirens, lodged himself outside our window early on a Saturday morning and shrieked, "I hate you," at his mother, the only thing that kept Joe from rushing out in his underwear to strangle him was my reminder that the whole Granly family would be leaving in another month.

And when Peter's mother, who was an obvious descendant of Job, launched into another description of the pain that led up to her hemorrhoidectomy, it was comforting to know that in a matter of weeks I'd be free, and some poor soul at a base in Georgia would be listening to the efficacy of sitz baths.

Still it was often difficult too. For close friendships as well as close hatreds were made quickly. So once I'd found someone who shared my hatred for women's bridge clubs and my determination to avoid all organizations with regular meetings and committee reports, I hated to see her go.

We moved in on the first of June—Joe, Vicar and I. Felicia had stayed behind with the Ohrbecks. I hated to leave her in the passionate paws of Badger, but base rules stated that all pets must be kept on a leash, and since the neighborhood was overflowing with dogs, it seemed best to let her stay where she was.

Would that we'd done the same for Vicar. For though he was loyal to a fault, and eminently serious about his duties as guardian and protector, he simply wasn't of a military turn of mind. He didn't sit. He didn't heel. He never came when called. When we put him on an exercise chain and hooked him up to the clothesline, the first thing he did was wind himself around the post till he couldn't move. Then he alternately howled and barked till rescued.

The greatest part of his day, however, was spent in planning to escape. All I had to do was crack open the screen door and reach a hand out to get the mail, and he bolted out and took off down the street with either Joe or me galloping after him.

I should have suspected he felt this way the day we moved in. For when we got out of the car he bounded into the house, raced from room to room, his toenails clattering on the bare floor like a swarm of click beetles, then took off out the back door. We were waiting for the delivery truck from Aurleigh's at the time, so we let him go, and trusted he'd come back on his own and not in an Air Police car.

Aurleigh's was a department store in town. It wasn't *the* department store. It didn't carry Chippendale desks and Persian rugs. But then it didn't sell sideboards in do-it-yourself kits either. It catered more to those of us in the middle whose taste was not to exceed our budget.

Joe and I had gone down there the previous Saturday. We had our list with us. It was long, covering everything from bedroom furniture to clothespins and a welcome mat. I could hardly wait to start, to saunter from department to department saying, "Yes, we'll take one of these, two of those, and if it wouldn't be too much trouble, one of those over there."

My eagerness must have shown. We'd barely walked into the furniture department when a salesman bounded over.

"Hiya there, folks," he said. "And what can I do for you good people today?"

He was tall and bony with a weatherbeaten look that suggested he spent his off hours buffeting dust storms. His string tie and fringed leather jacket furthered the image.

"Yes, sir," Joe said. "We're looking for a few things to furnish our new home."

The "sir" had given him away. Even I would have known Joe was military, and the salesman, a typical believer in the myth that military meant money, flashed an avaricious smile and stuck out his hand.

"You bet you," he said. "You've come to the right place. I'm Wilton Wooding, and I'm here to help you. Now, where shall we start?"

Selecting a couch seemed a good place, especially as we were up to our kneecaps in couches at the time. Wilton liked the early American number with ruffles and skirts and a print of brown coffee pots and orange spinning wheels.

"No, I don't think so," I said. "I'm not much on early American. It needs too many doodads and dust catchers to go with it."

"Right you are, little lady," he said, now dismissing early American as beneath contempt. "I'll bet this is more what you're looking for."

He was pointing to a leather monster with wagon wheel arms and cattle brands on the cushions.

"No," I said, searching for a way to phrase my objections. "That's a bit too, too masculine."

"Right you are little lady," he said again. "How about this?"

"No."

"Or this?"

"I don't think so." I looked over to Joe for help. I should have known better. Joe does not shop well. He says it's having to choose. It panics him. I believe him. I've since seen him in action, Christmas shopping. He edges in the front door of a store, gets a wild deer-surrounded-by-hunters look on his face, immediately buys two or three of whatever is closest, begs the saleslady to wrap them, and flees.

I was not about to let him flee then, not with Wilton breathing down my back. "Which one do you like, honey?" I asked.

He stared at me, stricken. "I . . . I . . . I don't know. How about this one?"

It was plain and gray. There were no carved legs, no cattle brands, no fringes of lace.

"We'll take it," I said.

Wilton blanched, then recovered his composure. "Excellent choice," he said. "In fact I was going to suggest it. Now what's next?"

"Next?" I was getting into the swing of it now. "Let's see. Next is a coffee table, and end tables too of course." I sailed into the adjoining department, and before they could catch up with me chose exactly what I wanted. They were step tables, popular at the time. I would later refer to them as a prime example of my early *Let's*

71

Make a Deal period. But at the time they seemed gorgeous.

From then on there was no stopping me. I chose a dining room table and chairs, not unlike those Mrs. Mackie had won. I picked out a washing machine with hot and cold cycles and two different water levels. And I selected some lamps, including a treelike number that extended to the ceiling and had swivel spotlights here and there.

"Now," Wilton exuded, flipping to page three of his order pad, "all that's left is finding what you want in the way of a bedroom suit."

"Suit?" I said. "Don't you mean suite—bedroom suite."

"That's what I said, little lady, a nice comfortable bedroom suit."

I opened my mouth to challenge him again, but Joe poked me and glared. So I shut it again, and we traipsed into the bedroom-suit section where we picked out a "gen-u-ine simulated walnut-veneer bookcase bed with dresser to match."

"And that," I said, as he marked "Sold" on the ticket, "is about all the damage we can do today."

"You sure now?" He scribbled furiously. "Couldn't I interest you in some lawn furniture, or maybe a three-shelf bookcase?"

"No. We've bought enough. We'll have to do with brick and board bookcases for a while longer." I wandered off to browse while Joe took care of the delivery arrangements.

Once that was through, we edged out of the store with Wilton following close behind suggesting one last cut glass ashtray or wrought iron plant holder. Finally we reached the door. I opened it and slipped out.

"Thank you," I said. "Bye now."

"And bye to you good people." His eyes shone and the string tie bobbed at his throat. "Now y'all come back and see us now, heah?"

"Oh, we will, Mr. Wooding," I called, quickening my pace. "We sure will."

Now it looked as if we might have to, if only to get our furniture delivered. For though they'd promised to come before noon, the afternoon was winding down, and even Vicar had returned. Finally I spotted the truck lumbering down Nehls.

"Hey, Joe," I called, "here they come. Do you want me to take the dog out and hook him to the clothesline so he won't attack or escape again? That way you can show them where to put the stuff."

"OK," he called out from the closet, where he was hanging up the last of his uniforms. "Just give me a minute. I'll be right there." I grabbed Vicar's collar and snapped on the leash just as the men were coming up the walk. Suddenly he wanted to stay inside. Obviously the enemy approached, and he wanted to prove his prowess. I managed to drag him out the door and around to the back.

"Come on, you stupid animal," I muttered as I tried to catch hold of the chain with one hand and keep him from bolting with the other. "You have to stay out here till the funiture folk are gone. That's all there is to it. So hold still and let me get you fastened here."

"Having trouble?" said a voice behind me.

I jumped and turned around. It was our neighbor. At least I assumed she was. I'd seen her going into the house next door.

"Oh, you startled me," I said.

"I'm sorry."

"That's all right. I'm just trying to get this silly dog chained up so the delivery men from Aurleigh's can bring in our furniture."

"Oh."

"You see we've been living at an apartment in town, but when Joe, that's my husband, was assigned here permanently they let us come on base. And since we've only been married for six months, we didn't have any furniture. So we went downtown and . . ." I caught my breath. I sounded like someone on the witness stand. "Anyway," I said, shifting gears, "I have to keep Vicar here out of the middle of everything." I snapped the chain to his collar and stood up. "I'm Ann Combs," I said.

"Hi," she said, pulling her blond hair back and securing it with a clip. "I'm Marge Perkins. My husband, Ted, and I are your neighbors." She gestured at the duplex next to ours.

"Oh. Have you been stationed here long?"

"No, just a couple of months."

"Is he—your husband—in one of the schools?"

"No, he's a doctor up at the hospital."

I registered the impulse to make some inane comment about having a doctor in the neighborhood and turned my attention instead to Vicar, who had already twirled himself around the pole and was in danger of strangling.

"Say," I said, once I'd gotten him free again, "have you time for a cup of coffee or a drink? I'd like you to meet Joe."

"Oh, I'd better not. You two are busy what with unpacking and all, and I'm sure he doesn't want company."

"Sure he does," I said, far more exuberant about making friends than I was about straightening the house. "Besides," I added, "we didn't have much to unpack, and most of it's already done."

She glanced at her watch. "Well all right," she said. "Just give me a minute to leave a note for Ted and to put a casserole in the oven and I'll be over."

"Great. I'll go in and see if we have any ice."

Joe was somewhat startled when I announced we were having guests. He wasn't used to opening the mess before the camp was set up and all the tent flaps were in place. "But Annie," he protested, "we have to arrange the furniture, and put the rest of the dishes away, and . . ."

"Oh, come on," I pleaded. "It's time for a break anyway."

"Oh, all right."

He located a couple of glasses and wrenched an ice cube tray out of the tiny freezer. Then while I shoved the couch over against the wall and lined up the end tables, he made drinks and dug around in the cupboard for a box of crackers. By the time he found them Marge was at the back door.

"Hi," Joe said introducing himself, "come on in."

I liked her instantly. She was both clever and caustic, and I delighted in her irreverence for protocol and military tradition. I liked Ted too. He wandered over when he came home and found Marge's note. He complemented her perfectly. He was dark where she was fair. He was tall and slender where she was about my height and of average build. He was deliberate and droll where she was bombastic.

Joe relaxed after the first blanket apology for the way the place looked. "Tell me," he said, sliding the plate of crackers over toward Ted, "are you career or just in for the required tour of duty?"

74

Ted halted mid-reach. "Just the tour," he said emphatically. "You couldn't pay me to stay one week longer than I have to. I'm not cut out for life in triplicate."

This was pretty much the consensus among the medics at Sheppard. Not because the base hospital was different from any other base hospital. It was simply that most doctors, like Vicar, were not of a military turn of mind. They didn't sit. They didn't heel, and, except in a medical emergency, they resented coming when called.

Their wives, as a rule, were independent too, and Marge was a good example. She didn't have Ted's date of rank embroidered on a sampler in their living room. She wasn't yearning for an invitation to the general's wife's house for tea. She was a cellist for the local symphony rather than a Gray Lady up at the hospital, and she shared my aversion for wives' clubs of any kind, be they medical, missionary, or military.

"I look at it this way," she explained. "I have better things to do with my time than listen to extended arguments about what color to have in the centerpieces for the March luncheon."

"But according to *The Air Force Wife,*" I said, hoping but still unconvinced, "they string you up and demote your husband to airman basic if you don't join and volunteer to be on the entertainment committee."

"Don't pay any attention to that," she said. "That's pre–World War Two stuff."

"Annie," Joe broke in, "I told you exactly the same thing. Don't you believe me? My career and how it goes depends solely on what I do, not on whether you're the hospitality chairman for the wives' club."

"Hot damn," I chortled, finally convinced. "Now, who'd like another drink?"

After they'd gone, Joe and I rummaged around getting dinner. It was such a treat to have a spacious kitchen I felt like whipping up a three-course affair. In the confusion, however, we hadn't had time to stock the larder, so the entree was scrambled eggs.

"My, I liked them," I said, looking in the cupboards to see where I'd put the skillet.

"Yeah," Joe agreed. "I only hope the rest of the neighbors are as nice."

"Well, Marge says that the couple next door are a bit odd."

"Odd?"

"Yeah, strange. You remember him. He was the short man with the horn-rimmed glasses you were talking to this afternoon."

"Oh, yes. He told me I'd better be sure and keep Vicar chained up, because he looked like a killer."

"That's the one. Anyway, he's Willard Beemer. He's a dentist."

"Is that what makes him odd?"

"No. He's weird naturally. Also"—I handed Joe a carton of eggs—"his wife, Bunny, never wears a bra."

"She what?" He stopped with an egg in his hand poised and ready to crack.

"She doesn't wear a bra." I chuckled. "According to Marge, this is why most of the men on the block come home on time every night. They don't want to miss it when Bunny dashes up and down herding her two little boys home for dinner."

"I'll look forward to that." He cracked the egg. "What else did Marge tell you?"

"Well, she said we'll probably never meet Captain Bellini's wife."

"Why not?"

"He doesn't let her out a lot. He's one of those men who, when he says woman's place is in the home, means in the home. In fact I gather that hanging out the laundry is the highlight of her week."

"That's stupid. What about grocery shopping? Doesn't she have to go to the commissary?"

"Nope. He does it."

"Well, I guess if they're happy that way . . ." He started beating the eggs, and I split a couple of English muffins and put them in the broiler.

"Now the couple in the duplex," I continued, "are British. I think Marge said he's a flight lieutenant. Of course, being British, they pronounce it leftenant, but it's the same thing. Anyway Marge knows his wife, Midge, and says she's lots of fun. Apparently her favorite expression is 'Keep your pecker up, luv. Tomorrow's another day.' "

"Good Lord, is there anyone you didn't hear about?"

"I don't think so." I buttered the muffins and put them back in to keep warm. "Are you about ready with those eggs? If so, let's eat."

After dinner we cleaned up the kitchen, unpacked a few more boxes, then made up the bed and crawled in.

"Here we are, on base at last," I said as we turned out the light. "We have our own furniture, our own house, sort of, and our own gen-u-ine simulated walnut-veneer bookcase bed."

"Right you are, little lady. Right you are."

☆ ★ ☆ 8 ☆ ★ ☆

OPEN TUESDAY
THROUGH SATURDAY,
MOST OF THE TIME

Civilians lie awake nights gnashing their teeth and tearing at their hair because military bases have commissaries and base exchanges.

"My God, Beulah," they say with righteous indignation quivering in their throats, "Jack Anderson is right. Those Pentagon brass hats are squandering *my* tax dollars, and all so's the military can load up on thick steaks and cheap groceries. It's scandalous." They continue pounding their pillows and pulling at their blankets. "Downright scandalous."

They'd lose less sleep if they weren't imagining wide aisles, a panoply of lettuce heads and artichokes, and sides of beef waiting to be hauled away for pennies a pound.

For commissaries are not the wonderland of shallots, marinated palm hearts, and escargot shells most people think they are. As a rule, and the commissary at Sheppard was no exception, they have all the luxury of a high school gymnasium, all the warmth of an inmates' grievance committee, and all the variety and selection of a Russian co-op.

Besides, the commissary isn't something you drop in on whenever the mood strikes. There's a ritual involved in shopping there. It's one I kept forgetting when we moved out to the base and I took over the grocery detail.

First, it's essential you check the calendar before you even consider venturing forth. If it's payday, make do with what you have at home. Serve Rice Krispies for dinner if you have to. Breakfast on hot dog buns and lemonade, but don't try to brave the commissary. For even if you make it in the door after spending the morning in a line that extends past the NCO club, you won't find much left on the shelves when you get there.

Second, be sure not to go on inventory day. The doors are closed and locked when it's time to take inventory. And in the Air Force, it seems, every time they run low on cream of mushroom soup, or the sergeant discovers they're out of paper napkins, someone announces it's time to take inventory again.

It's also not a good idea to attempt a grocery run during peak hours. Peak hours, in this case, are defined as any time when hordes of men in uniform may drop by to pick up a carton of milk or a bag of carrots. For the rule states, and it states it over and over again on official notices tacked to every post and wall, "All personnel in uniform are to go to the head of the line." Presumably this is so they'll get their groceries and get back to work. I've stood waiting for half an hour with a box of toothpicks in my hand while three-cart captains rattled by and coveys of nurses flocked up to the register ahead of me, all because, as they said, "We have to get back on duty right away."

After a while I realized the best time to hit the front door of the commissary is 0923 hours, except of course on Thursdays, when they open at 1200 and close at 1900, or on Monday, when they're closed because the checkers had to work on Saturday.

I also found that it's a good policy before heading in the door to stock up the larder to consider who's the commanding general these days. When we first moved to Sheppard it was General Green.

79

He was an easygoing sort, and a family man. Children under the age of twelve, therefore, were allowed to tag along while Mom did the weekly shopping.

By the time Joe and I had decided to enlarge our little group of Combses, the command had changed and General Stryder was in charge. He preferred dogs, Doberman pinschers in fact, to children. So he let it be known in no uncertain terms that children were to be banned from the commissary. I assume he feared they'd flop down in the aisles and start rolling cans of pork and beans at his ankles. Or perhaps he pictured babies flinging jars of puréed liver at field grade officers. Whatever his reason, children remained at home during his reign. Either that or they were bundled off to the day-care center to wait it out while Mother got the groceries.

The commissary at Sheppard was on the main street, about a block down from the officers' club, and maybe three blocks from our house. On days when I didn't have a lot to get I walked. It was a big box of a building, sitting on stilts, with steep wooden stairs leading up to the front door.

To be allowed in one had to go through the admission ceremonies. They rivaled those preceding entrance to a prohibition speakeasy. First there was the presentation of the ID card, then a quick glance from a bored airman to be sure I wasn't trying to sneak in in shorts, or with my hair in curlers. Both were forbidden by order of the Chief of Staff of the Air Force, the President of the United States, and, mostly likely, God.

Once in, I was allowed to take my place in the line waiting for a cart. The bag boys gathered them up as other customers went through the check-out line. When they had enough, or when they felt like it, whichever came first, they hooked them together and slid them across the floor at us. It was strictly one cart to a customer, unless of course you enjoyed being sworn at by those in line behind you.

After I had my cart, I could begin. The first section was fresh fruits and vegetables, not a good beginning. For rumor has it, and I personally started the rumor, that fresh produce in commissaries is whatever's left after the large grocery chains have swept through and taken the pick of the vine. I base this on the fact that the celery is usually pale and limp and it bends like a sapling in the wind. The little heads of lettuce huddle together and seem to shrivel up before your very eyes. The bananas are either kelly green or mottled with blotches of brown, and more than once in testing a cucumber I've had my thumb go right on through.

"You know what you need here?" I said one day in a vain attempt at banter with the surly man who was unloading cabbages. "You need a priest to give last rites to the green peppers."

He stared at me silently. But then I knew he would. For commissary employees do not laugh. Why should they? They were hoping for an assignment at the snack bar or in the motor pool. They're damned mad about pulling this duty and they don't care who knows it. This is why every time you mince up to the fellow who's shuffling chicken backs around in the poultry bin, and say, "Excuse me, sir. I don't mean to bother you, but would you be so good as to tell me if there will be any more hamburger in today?" he'll fix you with a stony stare, bark, "Hamburger's due Thursday," and leave.

Also if you approach the man who's adding another dozen boxes of frozen okra to the already plentiful supply, and dare to ask for asparagus spears, he'll shrug and say, "Search me, lady." He'll then rush to the back for today's shipment of collard greens.

It's a commissary rule: Never run out of okra and collard greens. No matter what the season, no matter where the base, be it Tachikawa, Wiesbaden, or Mountain Home, Idaho, let the stock of string beans lapse. Let the supply of broccoli dwindle, but never, never have less than a case of okra and collard greens.

I soon learned another lesson when I began my career as a commissary shopper. Have a list. Don't say to yourself, "Oh, well, I'll follow my usual route. That way I should find everything I need." This is because they change things around a lot. I suspect they do it when they've closed for inventory and find everything's already been counted.

This is why one week the taco shells and the enchilada sauce are next to the egg rolls and the breaded shrimp, and the next they're hiding at the end of the Kleenex and paper towel aisle. Sometimes when things have really been slow and the commissary officer is bored, they'll decide to shuffle things up completely, putting one size of frozen orange juice next to the eggs, another in a row with the TV dinners, and a third by the Sara Lee cheesecake. Supposedly this turns shopping into an adventure as you say, "Son of a gun, here's the one I want. Now all I have to do is dig out the other size and take it back."

Once your cart is full and you've made a note you'll have to get the onion rings, the furniture polish, and the Swiss cheese somewhere else, since the commissary's out, it's time to get in line for the checkout counter. This can take some time. You have to retrace your steps past the pickles and Ovaltine, past the tuna fish and dog food, past the kidney beans and sauerkraut, till finally you find someone who looks as if she's the end of the line.

"Are you waiting?" you say as you swivel your basket around trying to keep from knocking down three rows of cream style corn.

"I sure am," she answers, "and it looks as if we're going to be here for a while."

She isn't making idle threats either. Since only three of the ten cash registers are open, and one of the three has a trainee at the controls, the progress is slow. So slow in fact that by the time you get up to the front, you've had time to have an affair with the man behind you, and have exchanged life stories with the lady ahead.

Finally, however, you round the last bend and prepare for checkout. It's complicated, and at first I had to be reminded of the procedure.

"Keep your cans together," the cashier would snap as I unloaded my groceries. "Unless you want them on top of your bread."

"Oh, of course. I'm terribly sorry," I'd mumble.

"And face the prices toward me. I haven't time to search for them."

"I should say not. Please forgive me."

"That'll be $27.36."

I'd dig into my purse and extricate my checkbook. "May I write this for thirty-five dollars?"

"You can write it for anything up to ten dollars over the purchase," he'd say in a voice that suggested I was perhaps the only person on earth who didn't know this.

So I'd write, and he'd ask for my ID, and my address, and Joe's service number, and our phone number. And I, forgetting commissary employees do not laugh, would chuckle and say, "I'll tell you anything but my weight and age." He, of course, would glare and shuffle through a sheaf of papers checking to be sure my name wasn't on the deadbeat list. Then finally I'd be finished.

"Some days I wonder if it's worth it," I told Marge one morning when I struggled home scant hours after I'd left. "They were out of brown sugar, chicken breasts, and peanut butter; and the bag boy dropped my eggs, so I had to leave everything and go back to get some more."

She nodded. "I know what you mean," she said, pouring me a cup of coffee. "I went up yesterday for a bag of potatoes and some pork chops. But when I got to the check-out counter they announced my ID card had expired." She sat down. "Boy, you'd have thought I was trying to smuggle classified documents in the lining of my jacket. They brought Lieutenant Bussmeir over. You remember him. He's the manager, the one with no eyebrows. Anyway, they had a big conference, with half the store giving an opinion, and only when I promised to get the card renewed within a week did they let me take my measly purchases and go."

"Oh, Lord, how embarrassing."

She stood up. "Oh, that didn't bother me. What I do care about is this." She opened up the refrigerator and handed me a package of pork chops. "Look at these," she said. "Just look at these. They're green."

She was right—they were, around the edges and by the bone. They were a moldy green.

"What are you going to do?"

"What can I do?" She put the package back before it walked back by itself. "I'm not about to waltz back and tangle with Lieutenant Bussmeir, not with my ID still expired. And if I wait till I get my new one, they'll say the meat was fine when I bought it, and I simply left it out to rot."

I took a sip of coffee. "Why don't I take it back?" I said.

"You?"

"Sure. I'll just say I bought those chops."

She grinned. "Oh, would you?" she said. "I hate to put you to

83

the bother, but with the price of meat these days, it's criminal to see the money go to waste."

"No trouble," I assured her. "No trouble at all."

That was what I thought.

I went back up to the commissary that afternoon.

"May I see your ID?" The checker at the door eyed the chops suspiciously.

"Sure. I have it right here." I rummaged around in my purse, brought it out, and held it out for inspection. "Say," I said, "maybe you can help me." I showed him the pork. "I bought these here this morning and it wasn't till I got home and started to put things away that I noticed they're spoiled. So I thought I'd bring them back and get a refund."

"A refund?" He sounded as if I'd suggested kinky sex.

"Um-hm." I laughed a hollow laugh. "I've kind of lost interest in having pork chops after staring at these."

His suspicions were deepening. I could tell. "I'll tell you what," he said. "If you can wait while I check these ID's, I'll go get Lieutenant Bussmeir."

"Fine." I stood aside and tried not to look as guilty as I was beginning to feel. Finally he signaled someone to come and take his place. Then he led me back to the office.

"Lieutenant?" he said to a redheaded man leaning back in his chair. "This lady says she got these pork chops here this morning and they're no good."

Lieutenant Bussmeir got up. Marge was right. He didn't have any eyebrows, or at least they were so light he looked as if he didn't. I tried not to stare as he took the package and the airman went back to his work. "So," he said, motioning me to sit down, "you bought these here this morning?"

"That's right."

"Now Mrs. . . . ah . . . ah . . ."

"Combs."

"Yes, Combs. Now Mrs. Combs, you do know that regulations state any purchases you make are final once you've left the premises?"

"No, I didn't know that."

"Yes, I have it right here." He began searching through his drawer.

"But I didn't realize they were spoiled till I got them home. Surely you wouldn't expect me to walk out with a package of pork chops I knew were rotting, just so I could come back later."

He frowned. "Let me look at these again." He studied them as if waiting for a message to appear on the plastic wrap. "Well," he drawled, "I'll tell you what. These do appear to be a little—er—uh—discolored. But in order to be sure they're unsafe for consumption, I have to have the vet inspect them first."

"The vet?" I said. "Why the vet?" And then because I never learn I added, "Don't tell me this was a patient of his who didn't make it."

He was not amused. "It's regulations, ma'am. The vet has to inspect all commissary meat. So if you'll leave these with me, I'll have him take a look at them to determine if they truly are spoiled."

"And what do I do?" I asked, not really wanting to know.

"You give me a call in a couple of days, and if he agrees that the meat is no good, you can come up and get your money back."

"Chees," I said, "wouldn't it be simpler just to give me my money back now?"

"Sorry, ma'am, regulations."

So I went back home and told Marge the vet would have to pass on her pork chops, since her good friend no-eyebrows wasn't allowed to make that sort of decision on his own.

The next day I called the commissary.

"Base commissary, Sergeant Longley, sir," a voice snapped in my ear, and I resisted the impulse to ask him if there wasn't a fifty-fifty chance it might not always be a "sir" calling.

"Yes," I said, "this is Mrs. Combs. Is Lieutenant Bussmeir in?"

"No ma'am. I'm sorry. He's not in today."

"Oh . . . then maybe you can help. You see, I left a couple of rancid pork chops up there yesterday, and Lieutenant Bussmeir was going to have the vet inspect them and tell me if I could get my money back." I waited.

"I'm sorry, ma'am, I can't give out that information over the phone."

"What do you mean you can't give that information out? I'm not asking for plans for the H-bomb. I just want to know if I can get my money back."

"I'm sorry, ma'am." And he hung up.

I reported back to Marge.

She was apologetic. "I'm sorry," she said, "I didn't think it would be this complicated."

"Don't worry. Just remind me to check with that idiot lieutenant tomorrow."

"Oh, I will, never you fear."

But she forgot, and I forgot, and it wasn't till the next week when I went to get some flour and sugar that I suddenly remembered the infamous pork chops.

"Ah, Lieutenant," I called out when I saw him conferring with someone over by the salad dressing. "Remember me? The lady with the pork chops?"

"Oh yes, Mrs. . . . Mrs. . . . ."

"Combs."

"Ah yes, Combs."

"Well did the vet inspect them?" I asked.

For a minute he looked blank. Then he clapped his hands together. "I'm sorry, Mrs. Combs. I called him, but he's on leave and won't be back till the first of the month. So I can't give you a final decision till then."

"Good Lord," I groaned, "are you serious? You're going to keep those damn things for another three weeks?"

"Now ma'am, there's no need to get profane. It's as I told you before . . ."

"I know. I know, regulations." I turned to go. "I'll see you in three weeks," I said, and I left.

Actually I would rather have forgotten the whole thing, but I felt I owed it to Marge. Besides, Joe by now was intrigued with the idea of Annie versus the system.

"You know," I told him, "you could settle the whole thing if you'd go up and yell at him."

"Are you kidding? No one listens when a lieutenant yells, especially another lieutenant. Besides, you're doing fine on your own."

A lot he knew. I rushed up to the commissary the week after the vet was supposed to have come back from leave. This time Lieutenant Bussmeir was cowering in his office. But I walked right on in.

"All right," I said, "what's the verdict? Did the vet look at my pork chops, and did he give you his official permission to refund my money?"

He shook his head. "I'm sorry, ma'am," he said, "but by the time he saw them, they were so rotten he couldn't tell what they'd been like when you bought them."

I stared at him. "Didn't you have them in the freezer?" I howled.

"No, ma'am."

"Why not?"

"I had them in the refrigerator."

"But for a month?" My voice was reaching the upper registers. "How on earth did you expect to keep them in the refrigerator for a month?"

"Had to, ma'am. You see it's . . ."

"Don't tell me. I think I know. It's regulations, right?"

"Right." He smiled weakly.

"Sir," I said, "would you like me to tell you what I think of regulations?" I took a deep breath, then changed my mind. It wouldn't do any good anyway. "Never mind," I said, and left.

"My God, Joe," I said that night, "to think our tax dollars are paying that nincompoop's salary. It's scandalous. Downright scandalous."

9

$$\star \ \bigstar \ \star \quad 9 \quad \star \ \bigstar \ \star$$

SUMMERTIME, AND THE LIVING IS STICKY

At last [I wrote to Mother sometime in early May] I'm going to find out what real summers are like. After all these years of waiting till the Fourth of July or the eighth of August or the second of September for the sun to shine, I'm going to have three, maybe four months of the kind of summer weather I've always dreamed about.

According to the local propaganda, folks here in Texas acquire their tans in May rather than late August. There's none of this standing around looking albinic till the monsoon season ends. No one here gallops outside at the first hint of a break in the clouds to flop down on the lawn and catch whatever rays of sunlight are available.

You in the Pacific Northwest may spend the summer in your thermal underwear, but I'm going to wear sleeveless dresses. I'm going to wash our blankets and put them away till October. I'm going to sleep with the windows open all summer long, not simply during the last week of July. I'm even going to swim and not worry about how I look when my lips turn blue.

In short, at last I'm going to be warm for days on end. Because though you may consider three days with the temperature over 85° a heat wave, here they don't even mention the weather till it's been two weeks since the mercury dropped below 99°.

88

By the middle of June I'd already amended my hymns of thermal praise. For it was hot. It was hot in the morning when we rolled out of a damp sticky bed. It was hot at noon when the wind was like a dragon's breath searing us around the edges. It was hot in the afternoon when the sun dropped like a live coal in the western sky and its rays beat in the front windows. And it was hot at night as we lay motionless on top of the bed waiting futilely for a murmur of a breeze.

Houses weren't air-conditioned then. Restaurants were. Public buildings and theaters were. But it was almost easier to stay out of them. For once we cooled off and the perspiration behind the knees and in the bend of the elbow had evaporated, we forgot how hot it was outside. Then when it came time to go back out, the heat swept over us like stifling tidal waves.

At home there was no way to get cool. I thought, for a while, cross ventilation might be the answer.

"Don't you think that might work?" I asked Joe as I raised up the windows and propped open the doors.

"I doubt it."

"Why?"

"Because even at night it's just as hot outside as it is in here."

"Then what about this? What if I put a tub of ice in front of the back door, so the wind blowing over it will blow cool?"

"You can try it, but I don't think it will do any good."

He was right. It didn't. Neither did pulling the blinds, or soaking my wrists in ice water. There seemed simply no way to get cool. So we adapted. We grazed on lettuce and spinach salads, and at dinner called sandwiches the entree. We showered morning, noon, and night. We set out the sprinkler and chased each other through it. And we sat outside in the evening, battled mosquitoes, and talked to Marge and Ted till it was time to go in and try to sleep.

Sometimes thunderheads built up to the north, and we watched as the clouds billowed and surged, piling up on top of each other. Every now and then the storm would drift our way, so we'd grab our chairs and run for the porch, while the rain slashed out of the sky and bounced off the pavement. In twenty minutes it would be over, and the heat would return.

The neighborhood was busy that summer, with moving vans driving up and pulling away every other day. The Bellinis moved out sometime in July. Joe still hadn't met Mrs. Bellini, though I'd run into her twice at the clothesline. Two days after they left, Bob and Phyllis Walker moved into their quarters.

They were recently from a three-year tour in Hawaii, and the shock of trading sandy beaches, bougainvillaea, and the gentle ocean breezes for dust storms, tumbleweed, and tornado alerts was almost more than Phyllis could stand.

"If there were at least some trees around," she wailed one afternoon when Marge and I were out in the back yard trying to start some coals in the barbecue. "Just one or two to give some shade."

"Oh, there were," Marge said.

"There were?"

"Heavens yes. Last spring the base commander decided the whole place needed a little sprucing up. So he requisitioned fifteen hundred small trees and had them planted all over the base and the housing area."

"What happened to them?"

"Well, it went this way," Marge explained. "First a crew came out and dug holes. There were two in your yard," she said to me. "We had a couple, and there were some . . . Oh, they were all over the place, and they were huge."

"The trees were huge?"

"No, the holes were huge. In fact they looked as if they could house the root system of a full grown sequoia."

"Then what happened?"

"Nothing at first. In fact nothing for about a month. Of course all the kids in the neighborhood used them as foxholes for intricate games of war. And every time it rained they filled up with muddy water, and one child or another fell in. The Beemer boys fell in twice, and bra-less Bunny jumped in to save them." She chuckled. "Boy, that brought the local men stumbling out of their houses. And as I remember, old weird Willard threatened to sue the government, for endangerment or some such charge. Anyway, finally, one day they brought the trees."

"What kind were they?"

"Who knows?"

"What do you mean, Who knows? Couldn't you tell by looking at them?"

"Not really. They were so small and so scraggly, with only a leaf or two per tree, it was like trying to determine the sex of newborn kittens."

"Well then what happened?"

"They died."

"All of them?"

"All of them. And as fast as they died a maintenance crew was dispatched to replace them and the whole process started over again."

"Right from the digging of the holes?"

"Right from there. We fooled them, however. For as soon as each tree died we'd whip it out and cover the whole mess over."

"Didn't they object?"

"Naturally. Orders came down from above that all dead trees were to be left where they were and not tampered with. But since the grass had already grown up around them it was easy to wipe out all trace of where they'd been, and finally they gave up."

Phyllis sighed and lifted her hair off the nape of her neck. "Boy I wish they'd lived," she said.

Poor Phyllis. She was in agony. Finally Bob bought her an air conditioner for their bedroom, and like a bear going into hibernation she retired to her room during the day and only came out in the evenings.

I tried to urge Joe into the same arrangement for our house, but he resisted.

"It's not that I don't want to," he explained irrefutably. "It's simply that we can't afford one right now."

"Not even a teeny, tiny one?" I cooed, batting my eyes and trying to whip up whatever wiles weren't languorous from the heat.

"Not even a teeny, tiny one."

That was Joe's modus operandi. He started with a flat "no," hoping that would be that. He then worked his way through "maybe," "we'll see," "perhaps," and "let me think about it," till finally, when he was convinced I'd given up, he graciously, benevolently even, changed his mind.

91

This time he waited at least a week. Then one night at dinner when I announced I'd found a new way to cool off and hauled out a tub of water, directing him to put his feet in it, he relented.

"I've been thinking," he said, flinching and drawing back his feet before I could plunge them into the water. "You know what we need?"

"What?"

"An air conditioner."

I resisted the impulse to do handstands, lest too much exuberance at this point cause him to rescind his offer.

"Now nothing fancy," he continued, "but I've been looking around, and I know where we can get a good deal on a used evaporative cooler."

"Oh?"

"Yes. A sergeant at work has one for sale, and what's more he's offered to come over this weekend and help me put it in."

"Really?"

I jumped up, rushed over to give him a hug, and in the process stepped in the tub and knocked it over.

"Really?" I said again when we'd mopped up the mess. "Are you sure?"

"Of course I'm sure." He wrung out a towel, bent down, and wiped up the last of the water. "What's even better," he said, "is that he's selling it to me cheap, even though it's almost new."

"I wonder why?"

"Why what?"

"Why he's selling it cheaply."

Unfortunately we didn't ask. We soon found out however. It was because the sergeant had found out through sad experience that though evaporative coolers are fine in the desert, they were not meant for Wichita Falls weather. Joe explained it to me much later. It had something to do with the fact that evaporative coolers add moisture to the already humid air. I didn't quite understand the particulars. I did find out, however, that there was a price to pay for being slightly cooler.

For one thing this machine was not about to content itself with sitting in the bedroom window humming softly to itself. Not at all.

It had been told to cool, and by God it was going to cool.

We put it in the east window, the one directly across from the bedroom door.

"This is so the cool air will circulate into the living room too," Joe explained.

Circulate? That was a mild description. It raged. It blustered. It stormed like a misbegotten hurricane, and sent books, papers, and anything else carelessly left on the dresser soaring into the living room. It got so I had to dress in the bathroom and comb my hair in the kitchen to keep from looking like a disaster victim waiting for the local Red Cross.

Sleeping in the bedroom was like sleeping at the end of a runway. It was cooler all right, but the noise was so ferocious we couldn't hear anything. A squad of police cars with sirens wailing could have roared by the front door. Guerrilla warfare could have erupted on the side lawn. A helicopter could have landed on the roof and we would have missed it all.

Even Vicar's 4:30 A.M. salute to the paper boy, which normally bolted us both straight up in bed with our eyes snapped open, went unnoticed.

Then one day I noticed another side effect. The dresser drawers, swollen like sponges, were sticking shut, and all our shoes were starting to mold. Not only the shoes, but anything else made of leather. Our books took on a gray and fuzzy cast. My purses smelled as if they'd spent the winter in someone's dank and musty basement. Even my belts, hanging on their hook in the closet, looked like gray velvet ribbons.

"It's like living in the doldrums," I told Joe one morning as I wiped off my shoes and tried to pry open my dresser drawer. "What if you and I start to mold? I feel like that man in the Alfred Hitchcock story who ended up looking like a 'great, gray sponge.' "

"Oh, come now," he said. "Don't be so dramatic. All you have to do is put all this stuff out in the sun for a day. Wipe everything off and stick it out in the sun."

"What about the dresser? Shall I toss it on my back and carry it out too?"

"Don't be smart." He was on his way to work and in no mood

for sarcasm. "The dresser will dry out in the winter, but in the meantime get the rest of these things out in the dry air."

So I did. I lined them up on the sidewalk outside the back door, and Willard Beemer, who'd come over to complain because he'd stepped in one of Vicar's deposits that I'd missed on my morning "policing the grounds" expedition, looked at the assortment and said, "If you throw in a few woven blankets and a basket or two, you might get a good price for this junk."

I laughed through clenched teeth, considered telling him what I thought of grown men who stepped in things, and decided against it.

"I don't know what there is about Willard," I told Marge that afternoon when she was helping me take things back in the house, "but everything he does annoys me."

She laughed. "I know what you mean," she said. "Weird Willard is not your basic lovable tooth technician."

"He certainly isn't. I don't know how Bunny stands it. No wonder she doesn't wear a bra. She probably ripped it off in frustration when he issued one of his edicts. Do you realize," I said, sitting down on the back steps, "that he was bragging to Joe the other day because he didn't help Bunny move all their furniture around?"

"What do you mean?"

"Well, apparently she wanted to change the arrangement, and he didn't. So, as he said, 'I told her if she wanted it rearranged she'd have to do it by herself. I wasn't about to lift a finger to help her.' "

Marge nodded. "That sounds like Willard, all right. Last week when I was practicing the cello and Ted went out to bring in the laundry, Willard sauntered up and said, 'Doing woman's work, are you? If Marge were my wife, I'd make her quit all that screeching and squawking in there and tend to her chores.' "

"What did Ted do?"

"Nothing." She stopped. "Say," she said, "speaking of cellos, which reminds me of the symphony, are you still looking for a job?"

"Yes, off and on, why?"

"Because the business manager at the symphony's leaving, and they're looking for another one."

"But I don't know anything about symphony management."

"So, you can learn. It can't be too complicated."

"But Marge," I stuttered.

"But what? You're looking for a job anyway. And here's one available that certainly beats waiting on tables or being a sales clerk."

"Still . . ."

"Still nothing. You can stay at home dusting and vacuuming and scooping up after Vicar, or you can try to get a job that's interesting."

"True."

"And surely you don't object to earning money."

"No, but—"

"But, nothing. I think it's a great idea. You're intelligent, competent—"

"Careful," I warned, embarrassed at her compliments. "You're liable to run out of sterling qualities."

She laughed. "You'll do it then?"

"I don't know," I said. "Why don't you apply?"

"Because I can't play in the symphony and manage it too."

"Oh." I thought a minute. "But what would I do?" I asked. "I can't just go downtown, present myself at the symphony office, and say, 'Here I am, what you all have been looking for.'"

"Don't worry about that. I'll call Cliff Russell, the present manager, and set up an appointment for you."

"OK." I took a deep breath. "Don't tell Joe though, 'cause if I don't get it he won't have had his hopes raised, and if I do"—I felt a tingling sensation—"I'll surprise him."

"Good idea." She got to her feet. "Well," she said, "I'd better get in and start dinner. I'll let you know when I've talked to Cliff."

"Thanks. See you later."

Keeping secrets is not my forte, and it took all my will power that evening to stay silent. The next morning Joe left as usual, and I congratulated myself on my strength of character. I'd done the dishes and was putting in a second load of wash when Marge bounded over.

"It's all set," she said.

"You mean you talked to him?"

"Yep, this morning." She sat down. "Now I was wrong about

one thing," she said. "Apparently the manager's job has already been filled. They're bringing someone in from somewhere in the Midwest—someone who's gone to manager's school or something. But," she emphasized, "they need a secretary, since the old one quit, and Cliff wants you to come down this afternoon so he can talk to you."

"This afternoon? Oh, Lord."

"Now what's the matter?"

"Other than I'm a rotten typist, and don't know shorthand? Not much."

"Don't worry about that. You can pick it up." Her confidence in me was unending.

"But what about getting the car?"

"Isn't Joe coming home for lunch?"

"Sure, he always does."

"So, tell him there's a sale downtown and you need the car."

"I guess I could do that." I paused, planning what I'd say. "In fact that's exactly what I'll do."

It was easier than I thought, and once I'd taken him back to work, and sorted through every piece of clothing in my closet looking for a suitable but informal outfit, I got in the car and headed out the gate.

Cliff Russell was already in the coffee shop when I got there. He was a tall man, dark and in his mid-thirties. I gathered from his gentle soft-spoken manner that he wasn't an oil-well, cattle-ranch Texan.

He ordered two coffees and we found an empty booth.

"What we need," he explained as we sat down, "is someone to answer the phone and take care of the correspondence, that sort of thing. Then of course there's the fall subscription campaign. You'd be responsible for keeping all that straight. And I thought with your creative background, you might be able to work with the new manager on promotion ideas and such."

I wondered what he meant by my creative background. Obviously Marge had not been frugal with her adjectives. I also wondered if she'd mentioned my considerable lack of secretarial skills.

"You do know," I offered tentatively, "that I'm not much of a typist, and even less of a dictation taker, don't you?"

He waved that aside. "Don't worry about that," he said. "Dr. Kohary is Hungarian and fairly new to this country, so he dictates slowly. As for me I like to type out my own first draft. So there wouldn't be any problem there, at least not while I'm still here. The new man can do what he likes, but there's not a great deal of correspondence anyway."

He flagged down a waitress and asked for more coffee. "The main thing is," he continued when she'd refilled our cups, "we want someone who knows what a symphony is, and we want someone who can work well with members of the board when they come into the office from time to time. And I'm sure you wouldn't have any trouble with that."

I took a sip. "Does this mean I have the job?" I asked.

"If you want it," he said. He then went on to give me the particulars on hours, salary, and vacation time.

I barely listened. I've got a job, I thought, a real job. To hell with *The Air Force Wife*. This is going to be fun.

"And so," Cliff said, finishing, "I'll see you at nine on Monday."

"I'll be there." I shook his hand and refrained from kissing his feet. "And thank you," I added.

"Don't thank me," he said. "I'm delighted. See you."

Joe was already home when I got back.

"Well, well," he said when I walked in the door. "Did you have a good time? Did you buy out the store?" He looked for packages. "Where's the loot?" he asked. "I thought you went to a sale."

"Not quite. Actually I went on a job interview."

"A job interview?"

"Yes."

"Where? With whom?"

"Downtown, with the Wichita Falls Symphony. They need a secretary."

"A secretary? But I thought you told me you didn't know the first thing about being a secretary?"

"Ah, yes, my dear, I did," I said, rolling the words off my tongue. "But I do know how to spell Beethoven, and I got the job."

97

☆ ★ ☆ 10 ☆ ★ ☆

TAKE A LETTER,
IF YOU CAN

As far as I'm concerned, the only thing more awe-inspiring and mysterious than a composer who hears a symphony in his head and is able to transfer the notes to paper is a secretary who hears a letter dictated and is able to type it up with everything centered, all margins equal, and only an occasional "beofre" instead of "before."

I had a fair idea of my secretarial deficiencies when I arrived at work at eight forty-five on Monday morning. I knew, for instance, that no matter how many times I looked up "occasionally," I would never remember whether there were two "c"s and one "s," or one "c" and two "s"s, or two of everything including "n" and "l." I knew that my typing speed, a supersonic 32 words a minute, was not considered standard. And I knew I had to work on my centering skills, since most of the letters I typed looked as if they were either hanging on to the masthead, or slumped in a heap at the bottom of the page. But with the bravado of someone totally in the dark about the terrors ahead, I thought, Oh, well, I'll get the hang of it.

I would soon learn otherwise.

The symphony offices were downtown, on the second floor of the Hamilton Building. They consisted of two rooms: the manager's office and my domain. I had a desk, a chair that collapsed every now and then when I tried to skitter across the room to fiddle with the blinds, and several files.

I also had a phone, instructions to answer "Good morning, Wichita Falls Symphony. May I help you?" and a drawer full of stationery that would soon disappear in a flurry of hunt-and-peck and erase-and-crumple.

There weren't many offices along our hall. Aside from the one occupied by a large brooding man who claimed to own a herd of buffalo and bore a strange resemblance to his charges, the only other office on our side of the building was one intermittently visited by a geologist. There were a couple of storage rooms across the hall, and the ladies' room was down near the elevator, but that was all.

Cliff was already there when I arrived. He was working on the budget for the coming year, and after a brief tour of the pencil sharpener, the filing cabinets, the bulletin board, and the paper clip supply, he sat me down to project number one.

"What we have here," he explained, hauling out a large box of three-by-five cards, "is the alphabetized list of last year's season ticket holders. I think this is probably the best place for you to start." He opened up the box. "What I want you to do," he said, "is call each name on the list, ask them if they'd like to renew their subscriptions for the 'fifty-seven–'fifty-eight season, and make a notation of those who do and those who don't."

He flipped through some of the cards and showed me how it had been done in previous years. "There's no great rush on this," he said. "It's at least two weeks before the main campaign gets under way, but you might as well get a head start on things."

He headed into his office. "Oh, by the way," he said, "Dr. Kohary should be in later this morning. I talked to him last Friday, and he said he wanted to get some letters out."

I felt my confidence receding like an ocean tide, but I tried not to show it. "Fine," I said, in a tone I hoped sounded convincing. "That'll be fine."

Then I stuffed my purse in the bottom drawer of my desk and started to work.

It wasn't hard. "Hello?" I'd say. "This is Mrs. Combs from the office of the Wichita Falls Symphony. I'm calling to ask if you would like to renew your symphony tickets for the coming year."

"How's that?"

I'd repeat.

"Oh . . . well, I'll have to ask my husband. We didn't get to too many concerts last year. Bill was down with lumbago a lot last winter, you know."

"Oh, I'm sorry. Why don't I call back in a day or two when you've had a chance to talk to him?"

"That'd be fine, honey, just fine."

I'd hang up, put a question mark on the card and dial again.

Some people were insulted that I had to ask. "Why Mizz Combs," they'd drawl, "of course we want tickets. We support all the cultural activities here in town. Why we've been going to the symphony ever since it started."

Others said, "No thanks. I've already heard a symphony."

Mildred Fawcett sounded flustered when I called. "Could you wait just one minute, dearie?" she said when I identified myself. Then I heard a scrambling and a scratching in the background. Finally the pulsating strains of Ravel's Bolero filled the air.

"Now whom did you say this was?" she trilled into the phone.

"Mrs. Combs," I said, "from the Wichita Falls Symphony office. I called to ask if you'd like to renew your tickets for the coming season."

There was a pause while the Bolero throbbed like an amplified heartbeat. "Oh, my dear, of course I would," she said. "I simply love classical music. I listen to it all the time."

Perhaps she did. I doubted it though. Still, every time she called the office, and that was at least once a month, the Bolero was thudding in the background like an orgiastic giant.

Dr. Kohary came in around ten-thirty. I knew it was he the minute

I heard the elevator doors open at the other end of the hall.

He was not as I imagined. There was no wild shock of electric hair. No tattered jacket was slung carelessly over his shoulders. No trail of musical scores fluttered in his wake.

He was small, about five feet eight or nine, and slight, more like a maitre d' or a country squire than a symphony conductor. Everything about him was impeccable, from his tiny manicured mustache to his mirror bright shoes.

I stumbled to my feet when he came in, and my chair skidded out behind me, rolled across the floor and banged into the radiator.

Dr. Kohary blanched ever so slightly, and Cliff, ignoring the clatter, rushed to introduce us.

"Dr. Kohary," he said, "this is our new secretary, Mrs. Combs."

Dr. Kohary took my hand and bowed. "How do you do, Mrs. Combs," he said, his thick Hungarian accent embroidering the words. "I am delighted that you will be working with us here at the symphony."

The delight, I suspect, faded slightly in the next hour, for out of the first eight letters dictated, six had to be redone twice.

"But do not worry," he said, obviously noting the beads of nervous perspiration shimmering on my forehead. "I know that soon you will be much more. . ." He paused, searching for the right word, and "unemployed" flitted through my mind. "Much more . . . without mistakes," he concluded.

"Oh, I will," I blathered, "I will."

And strangely enough I did improve. True, I used up half of the office stationery in the first week or so, but after a while I was able to dash off notes to composers, other conductors, and guest artists in only one or two tries. By Christmas Dr. Kohary was even asking me to correct his English and smooth out any awkward phrases.

He came into the office fairly often to dictate letters, to check on arrangements for an upcoming concert, or to confer with Cliff. He was always cordial. He always asked after my health, and he was always gallant, insisting, "Ah, Mrs. Combs, please, let me lift that box. It is much too heavy for you to carry."

Should someone from the board of directors wander in to report on the latest attempts at fund raising, he became positively courtly. Especially if that someone was Mrs. Kinney.

She was our most frequent visitor. Her husband was one of the wealthiest men in town. Apparently he was a former college football coach who'd invested in a small oil venture that immediately became a large oil venture. By the time I met him he owned half of downtown Wichita Falls, and I think he was negotiating for the other half.

Mrs. Kinney was the backbone of the symphony, and while her husband traded Boardwalk and Park Place for three railroads and a utility, she tramped from Bill's Bowling Alley to the Branding Iron Cafe twisting arms and getting donations for the symphony. Every now and then she came up to the office.

"Mah stars," she said one day when she whiffled in out of the rain like the last stage out of Dodge City, "Ah've been so busy goin' from here to there and back again, ah haven't even had time to buckle up mah galoshes."

Dr. Kohary was there that day, and while the rest of us stood around and nodded, he dropped to his knees and did the honor for her.

Other board members came in from time to time. John Tower came in. At the time he was still a professor of government at Midwestern University. Lyla Mae Windburn, who claimed she'd always wanted to be a "celloist," came in. And Mrs. Thurmon came in. I always looked forward to her visits, if only for a change to gaze at all three karats in her diamond ring. She also kept us up to date on news of her son who had built a million-dollar estate just out of town. Unfortunately he'd built it on a rattlesnake nest, so spring afternoons were spent shooting at rattlesnakes on the front lawn.

In between all these visitations I kept busy calling ticket holders. It wasn't always simple. Two days before Tom Holder, the new manager, was due in I hit a snag.

I'd worked my way down to the N's. "Nersessian, Sam," the card said. I dialed his number.

"May I speak to Mr. Nersessian?" I asked when a woman answered.

"Which one?"

"Samuel."

"Oh, I'm sorry, ma'am. This isn't his office. Would you like me to give you that number?"

"Thank you. I'd appreciate it."

She rattled off a number. I noted it and dialed again.

"Hello?"

"Yes, may I speak to Mr. Sam Nersessian, please?"

"I'm sorry, he doesn't work at this office, but I can get his number for you."

"Thank you."

I waited while she looked it up. "Let's see," she said. "That's 723-8649."

I thanked her again, and hung up. Then it hit me. She'd given me the number I'd called originally.

"Cliff," I called out, "can you explain something here? I'm trying to get hold of Sam Nersessian. According to our records he's had season tickets for several years, so I wanted to be sure and get him, but the first number I called said he didn't work there, and then the second number . . ."

Cliff laughed. "Look at the next card," he said.

I looked. "Nersessian, Samuel," it said.

"I don't understand."

"It's simple. The Nersessians have four sons—Sam, Samuel, Sammy, and Willy."

"Willy?"

"Apparently they ran out of variations on Samuel."

"Oh." I shuffled through the cards again. "Doesn't it get awfully confusing though?"

"Not really. They're a well-known family, and most people don't even give it a second thought."

"Well, it's confusing to me." I put the cards back. "And I bet it'll be confusing for Tom Holder. Speaking of which," I said, "when exactly is he due?"

Cliff checked the calendar. "Monday," he said. "He arrives in town tomorrow night, has a couple of days to get settled, and should appear on the scene bright and early Monday morning."

"That doesn't give him much time to learn the ropes, does it?

Aren't you leaving at the end of the next week?"

"Yes, but don't worry." He patted me on the shoulder. "I'm counting on you to teach him. You and Dr. Kohary, and Mrs. Kinney."

I shook my head. "Poor thing," I said. "I wonder if he knows what he's getting into."

"Probably not. This is his first assignment as a manager. But at least he should be eager."

Cliff was right. Tom Holder was definitely eager. Sadly though, his eagerness was directed to posters and campaign slogans and luncheons with the Chamber of Commerce, not to correspondence with sheet music companies, phone calls to advertisers, or arrangements with the printers.

"You take care of that, Ann," he'd yell from the other office. "I'm busy right now." Then he'd go back to planning the layout for a handbill he thought might be catchy.

Tom was young, only two years older than I. He was a bachelor, recently graduated from college, and this was his first time away from home. Home was a small town in northern Wisconsin, light-years from Texas. And though he tried, the ways of Texans baffled him. But then the eccentricities of musicians frustrated him too. The demands of the board nettled him, and Dr. Kohary intimidated him.

I teased him.

"Come on, Tom," I'd say as he paced around the office, bumming his third cigarette of the morning, "you know you love these symphony guild meetings. They'll have coffee and little finger sandwiches, and they'll ooh and ah and ask you why a handsome fellow like you isn't married."

"Thanks a lot," he'd snarl, looking for yet another reason to delay his departure. "That really helps."

"Oh, don't be so stuffy. Just get going."

Tom liked to think he ran a taut ship. He lived by the myth that members of the orchestra jumped when he sent down a directive, and campaign workers waited breathlessly for his orders. I tried to dispel this notion. I also tried to persuade him to give me the afternoon off every now and then when things were glacially slow. But he would have none of it.

"What if someone should call?" he'd say. "What if Dr. Kohary decides to come in? How will it look if the office is closed and locked?"

"No one's going to call," I'd assure him. "And Dr. Kohary is still in New York."

But he wouldn't relent. So while the phone remained silent and the only signs of life on the whole floor were mumblings down the hall from the buffalo man, I either wrote letters, or sat in Tom's office with him and played poker with match sticks and paper clips.

He did relent slightly when, about a month after he came, I found out that, now that I was finally employed, I was also pregnant. And once my increasing girth proved the fact, he was even solicitous.

"Why don't you take off early," he'd say on a Friday afternoon at four forty-five. "You look beat."

"You're all heart, Tom," I'd tell him, grabbing my bag and my coat. "But I guess fifteen minutes is better than nothing, so I'll take you up on the offer. Goodbye."

Of course on concert days I could have been comatose and he would have insisted I stay at my post. For on concert day Tom was like an intern in the emergency room.

"Are you sure the piano tuner has been here?"

"Who's supposed to meet the guest soloist?"

"Where are the programs? They still have to be folded, you realize."

He stationed me at the ticket office in the auditorium.

"All right now," he'd say, jabbing his pencil at the seating chart. "These are the open seats, and these are the—"

"I know, Tom, I know. Who do you think made all those scribblings?"

"Oh, that's right. . . . Now don't forget, I've left two tickets over here for the Boardmans. They're my landlord and his wife."

"You already told me that, Tom. Now calm down. It's all going to be fine."

Luckily he left me alone for most of the day. Alone to wait for the herds of ticket seekers who never came. Sometimes Marge wandered down in the afternoon when they had a rehearsal. Dr. Kohary dropped by every now and then to leave a message or pick up a program. And Tom brought me a hamburger and coffee at lunch. But for the most part I was by myself, reading whatever I could find: the paper, the program, my book, the signs on the wall that listed the numbers to call in case of an emergency. Sometimes I wrote letters. I wrote to people I liked. I wrote to people I didn't like. I wrote to strangers. I wrote to companies and complained about the fiber content in their paper towels. When that paled I straightened up the ticket office one more time and tried to see if I could make up a musical crossword puzzle.

Things picked up around dinnertime. The musicians started to wander in. The telephone came to life with inquiries as to when the concert was scheduled to begin, and did we have any decent seats left. Tom always came in to fidget and pace and bum cigarettes and worry about whether or not the stage had been set up correctly.

Joe usually ate dinner at home and then came down for the concert. There was no use his offering to take me out. I couldn't have gone. I had to stay at my post and wait for Tom to deliver another hamburger and another cup of coffee.

Around seven-thirty, people started drifting in. It was quite a show. Full-length minks, satin evening gowns, tuxedos, occasionally jeans and hand-tooled boots. I sold tickets, answered the phone, gave directions to the coat room, and took messages.

Finally it was time. The doors closed. I could hear the orchestra tuning up, and then the overture began. I usually waited for half an hour or so, to intercept stragglers and ask them to wait till the first number had finished. Then I locked up the ticket booth and slipped in to stand at the back.

It was glorious there in the dark, with the music washing over me. Suddenly it didn't matter that "conductor" had been misspelled on the program, that Tom had forgotten to put a pitcher of ice water in Dr. Kohary's dressing room, that Mrs. Kinney had left her doeskin gloves in the office and I hadn't brought them over to the auditorium to give to her.

Suddenly the intricate travel arrangements for the guest soloist seemed worth it. It didn't matter any more that one of the violinists had a cast on her leg and was worried for fear her dress wouldn't cover it. And it seemed trivial that Mildred Fawcett had misplaced her tickets and thought we hadn't sent them.

The music soared. It whispered. It raged and thundered. Even Tom stopped his pacing and stood quietly at the back with me.

"Say," he said as the final notes died away and the audience broke into applause, "this has been a long day for you. Why don't you come in a little later tomorrow?"

"Why that's sweet of you Tom. Thank you. I will."

"Think nothing of it." He headed off to mingle with the crowd and accept his just due. "See you at nine-thirty."

11

AT LEAST THE PILGRIMS DIDN'T PLAY MAH-JONGG

Joe is not a devotee of aimless chatter. Even when it's aimed, he tends to duck and let it sail on by. I, on the other hand, will talk about anything, to anyone, at any time of the day or night. I'm one of those who answer the phone at two in the morning, insist they weren't asleep, and have a five-minute conversation with a drunk who dialed a wrong number.

Down at the office I swapped pleasantries with New York telephone operators who were trying to locate Dr. Kohary. I chatted with the buffalo man as we waited for the elevator and he explained the tribulations of owning bison. And I traded pre-natal complaints and superstitions with the waitress in the coffee shop who had three children of her own.

On slow afternoons when Tom was off somewhere getting poster paints or having coffee with a member of the board, I called Marge and regaled her with embellished stories of the Nersessian boys, or the guest soloist who caught a plane to Wichita, Kansas.

I even talked to weird Willard when I was out at the clothesline and he was skulking around the neighborhood looking for a cavity in progress. And when Vicar was safely locked inside the house I managed to exchange a few friendly words with the mailman. But with Joe it was another thing. My attempts at getting him to enter into a lively dialogue by asking, "How did things go today?" were usually thwarted with monosyllabic answers.

At first I took it personally.

"Are you mad at me?" I'd pout.

"No, why?"

"Because you won't talk."

"What do you mean I won't talk?"

"Just that."

"I'm talking now, aren't I?"

"That's not what I mean."

After a while it got too complicated to pursue.

I then chose to believe that he, as an intelligence officer and guardian of the national security, was simply privy to so many secrets he couldn't risk casual conversation about life at the office lest he divulge one. Joe fostered this notion.

"How's Nick these days?" I'd ask.

"Fine."

"Connie says he's off on a trip."

"Yep."

"Where'd he go, or should I ask?"

"Don't ask."

He went, as it turned out, to Albuquerque, to his brother's graduation. But when I confronted Joe and said, "You led me to believe he was off on a secret mission," he said, "If I'd told you he was going to his brother's graduation, you would have wanted to know why wasn't Connie going? How long was he going to be gone? Was he driving or flying? Did he have other brothers and sisters? All that sort of thing, and I was too tired to go into it."

Joe never has understood my thirst for trivial information. And when, after we'd been to an "attendance required" office party, I grilled him on what he and the other husbands found so amusing as they congregated up at the bar, he always said, "Oh, nothing much."

I hated those office parties. It was like déjà vu of dancing school.

Everyone was forced to come. Everyone was starched and polished. And the women always huddled in the corner while the men gathered at the bar.

The scenario never varied. Colonel Fenway, a man who looked as if perhaps he'd once been tall and then had had the misfortune to walk under a descending elevator, always came alone and stood brooding at the end of the bar. Apparently he once had been married. He even had grown children. But his affinity for bourbon and branch water had led to a stormy divorce. Now he contented himself with military matters during the day and dissipation in the evening hours.

He was a shy man, the sort who would rather cross the street than be forced into conversation. And though he believed a commander should be on a first-name basis with all his men, he never could remember their first names, so he simply called everyone George.

Wives were left nameless, and should one who was new to the base and not yet briefed on his idiosyncrasies sail across the room and try to charm him, he'd scurry behind the bar and hide till she was gone.

Colonel Samper, on the other hand, welcomed feminine attention. He invited it; insisted on it even. It was always he who was the first to break ranks with the men and wander over to the clutch of wives, hallooing and saying, "Well, and how are all you beautiful ladies this fine evening?"

No party was a success to him until he'd patted a few feminine fannies. The number of fannies and the choice of their owners depended on how many martinis he'd had. I usually placed seventh. But when my impending maternity became more and more apparent, I moved up to fifth. I was never quite sure why. Either he felt I was a safer target in my condition, or else he thought I'd be flattered at the attention. Either way I was unmoved.

Nick, his ever present deck of cards in his pocket, was always on the lookout for someone new who hadn't seen his floating diamond trick. Connie, however, refused to shill for him and turned her energies instead to fanning the flame already burning brightly in Charlie Moffit's soul.

Occasionally Joe came over to see if I was all right or if I needed another drink, but for the most part he stayed on his side of the room. This left me at the mercy of Mrs. Samper, who was determined I should join the wives' club. If she was proselytizing elsewhere, I could listen to Jan Epler and Maggie Donner trade tuna casserole recipes. I could hear about the traumas of birth and the ensuing post-natal depression from Wynn Kotz, or I could let Fran Moffit describe once more the time she made the seven-ten split and moved into first place in her bowling league.

We were a motley crew brought together only because someone had been reassigned or promoted, and every now and then I broke away and retreated into the ladies' room on the off chance that when I returned the crowd would have desegregated and livened up somewhat.

It was a mistake. The mirrored walls and fluorescent lighting in any standard ladies' room can make the most glorious of women look like an embalmer's practice dummy, and I was definitely not the most glorious of women. I tried to believe the propaganda about pregnant women and their special glow, but it seemed as I stood there in my blue brocade with the color drained from my face that the glow had eluded me.

Perhaps it was the blue brocade. Perhaps flaming red or burnt orange would have made me luminescent. I doubted it. It didn't matter anyway. Blue brocade was all I had. I'd intended to expand my wardrobe, but my sister-in-law had vetoed the idea.

"It's silly for you to go to all the expense of buying a lot of clothes," she wrote as soon as she learned I was pregnant, "especially when I have six or eight perfectly good outfits I can lend you."

I couldn't argue with that, so I put my checkbook away and waited for the mail. It was a long wait. Oh, she packed them up all right. But then she made a fatal error. She gave the package to my brother to mail. He had his mind on other things that day, and when he got to the post office he suddenly remembered he didn't have our address. So rather than be saddled with a large brown package all day he simply sent it off to: "Joseph Combs, Sheppard Air Force Base, Texas."

The mails were swift. Within the week the package was delivered to Joseph Combs—Joseph G. Combs—a lieutenant in maintenance.

111

Actually it wasn't delivered directly to him, for minutes before it arrived he was transferred to Korea. So it was forwarded.

And while Joseph G. Combs sat in Seoul and wondered who would play this kind of a sick joke on him, I waited in my blue brocade and wondered how many office parties I could wear it to before someone suggested they pass the hat and get me a replacement.

I'd thought of making myself something new. Joe had even bought me an inexpensive sewing machine. His motives were less than altruistic though, and his assessment of my talents were far from realistic. When we'd loaded it in the car, he'd turned to me with love and adoration in his eyes and remarked, "Say, now you can make my uniforms."

Obviously I'd neglected to tell him about my disastrous days in high school Home Ec when an entire term was spent trying to make a red and white striped dirndl skirt. By the time I finished I'd stitched and ripped and restitched and reripped so often the fabric was like gauze. And since I looked grain fed and corpulent in dirndl skirts anyway, my project was quickly converted into two dust cloths, a polishing rag, and a bird cage cover.

Time, however, had dimmed the memory of past inadequacies, and now while I waited for Joseph G. Combs to send my wardrobe back, I tried my hand at a few loose and simple maternity tops to tide me over till he did.

They were far from professional creations, and their display was limited to the commissary, the back yard, and occasionally, if most of the seams were straight and the collar lay flat, the office. My blue brocade, however, remained the uniform for office parties.

In fact the most grandiose occasion to which I dared wear a Combs original was Thanksgiving at the Gibbs'. Normally I wouldn't have risked it even then, for the dressiest outfit I'd made had one pocket higher than the other, a collar that puckered slightly in the back, and sleeves that didn't quite match. But since the fabric was dark I convinced myself no one would notice.

Besides, it wasn't as if we were invited as honored guests. This was to be a joint affair. Connie had called me in early November.

"It's ridiculous for you two to cook a turkey just for yourselves," she'd said. "So why don't we get together at our house. We can split the cost of the bird, and divide up the rest of the stuff between us."

It sounded reasonable to me. Marge and Ted were driving down to Dallas for a long weekend, so we wouldn't be sharing the holiday with them. And I still thought of cooking a turkey as a mystical rite akin to pressing a duck. So I agreed.

I had a few qualms later when I checked the list of what we were to bring. Connie had thought it would be nice if we brought the liquor for Bee's Knees, her latest passion; a couple of cartons of soft drinks for Donnie and their daughter, Chris; potato chips; a dip; and three kinds of pie. She and Nick, she assured us, would furnish the stuffing, sweet potatoes, and a salad.

"It doesn't seem quite even to me," I told Joe. But when he offered to call up and equalize the situation I stopped him. "No, don't," I said. "I guess we have to take into account the fact that it's at their house and Connie's doing the cooking."

I didn't believe it, but I didn't want to create a scene. Besides I'd been raised to think that not only the meek but also the stepped-on shall inherit the earth. So I bought potato chips and Coke. I mixed up a good sized bowl of onion soup dip. I picked up a bottle of gin and some lemon juice and honey, and I made pies. I tried to get away with only pecan and pumpkin, but Joe insisted on mince too.

"Please," he said. "Mince pie is my favorite, and Thanksgiving just isn't Thanksgiving without it."

So I gave in and made mince too.

Thanksgiving day dawned bright and sunny. Joe and I got up late, had a leisurely breakfast, then got dressed, straightened the house some, and loaded the car. Around noon we headed across town, and twenty minutes later we pulled up in front of the Gibbs'. Donnie greeted us at the door.

"Who are you?" he asked as he tried to stuff an entire banana into his mouth at once.

"The Combses," Joe said. "Is your dad around?"

Donnie nodded.

"Will you tell him we're here?"

He nodded again. Then he slammed the door shut. "Dad, Dad,"

we heard him call. "There's people at the door."

We listened for a reply. It was long in coming, but finally Nick opened the door. "Come in, come in," he said as he took the liquor and the Mah-Jongg set Connie had told me to bring along. "Just put the rest of the stuff right in the kitchen." He gestured. "It's right through there."

Joe carried the pies and I brought the rest.

"Hello there, you all," Connie trilled as we set them down. "You're right on time. Just make yourselves at home, and I'll be right with you."

She looked dramatic as usual in black velveteen pants and a pink angora sweater. She was up to her elbows in turkey stuffing, and when Nick came in to take our coats, she waved a saged and parsleyed hand at him.

"Mix up a batch of drinks, honey," she said, "and get out the Mah-Jongg. As soon as I stuff this little devil and stick him in the oven we can play."

"All rightee," Nick chortled. "Come on, you two. I'll just put these in the bedroom, and then we'll see what we can do to get this show on the road."

I waited till he was out of earshot. Then I poked Joe. "Shouldn't the turkey have been in the oven hours ago?" I whispered, remembering that Mother always got up at dawn because, as she said, "Turkeys take all day to cook."

He shrugged.

"After all, didn't she say it weighed twenty-five pounds?"

"I don't know," he said. "Surely she knows what she's doing."

"OK." And then because I could hear Nick coming back, I opened up the Mah-Jongg case and began taking out the tiles.

By the time Nick had made the drinks and I'd brought in the dip and chips, Connie was through, and the bird was safely in the oven. So we settled down on the floor around the coffee table and started to play. I checked my watch. It was one-fifteen.

By two the game was neck and neck. Joe had started off with a couple of winning hands, but Nick was catching up. I'd just drawn my fourth immortal for a second double and threatened both of them. Connie lagged behind. I think the three Bee's Knees she'd gulped like lemonade had taken some of the killer instinct out of her.

Every now and then Chris appeared at the living room door and announced Donnie was touching something, eating something, breaking something, or fooling around with something. Each time Connie called out, "Donnie, baby, you stop that now, heah?"

By three Joe had pulled back into the lead. Nick and I were tied for second, and we had to remind Connie it was her turn. Chris kept us current on Donnie's activities.

Finally when she informed us Donnie was feeding olives to the goldfish, Connie got to her feet.

"All right, all right," she said, swaying first one way and then the other. "I'm coming. I'm coming." Then she stumbled off down the hall calling, "Donnie? You'd better watch out. You've made Mummy upset."

I listened, hoping to hear sounds of corporal punishment, but all was quiet. Joe and Nick added up the score.

When they finished, Nick slapped his hand on the table. "Aha," he cried. "Finally. I'm ahead." He beamed. "That calls for another drink. What do you say, Ann? How would you like another drink?"

I'd been careful, nursing my second one and drinking coffee at the same time. "Not for me," I said. "Too many in my condition and I'll get sick, but you go ahead."

"All rightee, I think I will." He got up. "Come on, Joe, you need a refill too." He lumbered into the kitchen and lumbered right back out. "We're out of gin," he said in a tone that suggested it had evaporated while we played Mah-Jongg. "We're actually out of gin. Can you believe that?"

He scratched his head. "Wait," he said. "I know of a liquor store that'll be open. Come on, Joe." He tugged at Joe's arm. "You and I can go out and get some more booze while Connie's in rescuing the goldfish."

Joe pulled back. "Oh, I don't know, Nick," he said. "We're OK, aren't we?"

"OK? My boy, hours are going to pass before we can open up the wine for dinner, and I am getting parched."

Joe looked at me then looked at Nick. "Oh, all right." He patted me on the shoulder. "We'll be back in a minute. You stay here and keep Connie company."

Then he and Nick went out the door, closely followed by Donnie and Chris, who, it seems, had heard the magic word "store."

I sat down on the couch and picked up a magazine. Connie must be in the bathroom, I thought. I listened. There was no sound. I skimmed through an article about Christmas in Tasmania. Still no Connie. I tiptoed down the hall. The bathroom door was open. No Connie. I peered into the bedroom. There she was all right, sound asleep on the bed. Oh, great, I thought. Now what? I went back into the living room and waited for Joe and all to come back.

It was a long wait. Finally, however, I heard the car pull up. The front door burst open and Donnie and Chris rushed in. Joe followed, and then Nick.

"Damnedest thing," Nick announced as he came in. "I forgot to take my wallet. Luckily old Joe here had some money, didn't you, Joe?" He slapped Joe on the back and Joe gave me a sickly look. "Yep," Nick continued, "he even had enough for more Coke for the kids. So . . . now . . . let's mix up another batch of drinks and get back to our game." He paused. "Say, where's Connie?"

I pointed toward the bedroom. "She's asleep."

"She is?" He chuckled. "Old broad. She never could hold her liquor. Well, we'll let her sleep it off for another hour or so. But she better get up then," he said, "and get to cooking. After all, it's Thanksgiving."

I was tempted to tell him I'd give thanks when the whole blasted day was over, but I resisted. I didn't resist, however, when I saw him rummaging through the desk drawer and heard him ask Chris where her deck of cards was.

I jumped up. "I have an idea," I almost shouted with an enthusiasm usually saved for reactions to an engagement announcement. "Why don't we play three-handed Mah-Jongg. It's easy, believe me."

Luckily I was in time. So for the next couple of hours we shuffled tiles and built up walls.

At five-thirty Nick stood up. "Chris," he yelled, "go wake your mother and tell her it's time to get with it. The rest of you follow me. We are about to get dinner on the table." He loped into the kitchen, and we trailed after like obedient airmen on KP.

Joe was assigned potato peeling. Chris and I were to make the salad. "Be sure to tear the lettuce not cut it." Donnie was to stay out of the way. And Nick was to supervise.

I peered into the oven to see how the turkey was coming. It was still somewhat pale, so I basted it and eased the oven temperature up a bit. Nick came over to kibitz.

"My, doesn't that look scrumptious," he said.

"It sure does," I said, "but don't you think it needs a bit more cooking?"

"Nonsense," he roared. "By the time we have everything else ready it will have reached the absolute pinnacle of perfection."

"If you say so," I replied, and when he turned his back I eased the temperature up even more.

By the time Connie wandered in, the salad was ready and back in the refrigerator chilling, the potatoes were on to boil, and Nick had some green beans simmering. Connie looked dazed, as if she were peering through fog. One side of her face bore the imprint of her bedspread, and she flinched at the sound of dishes rattling and pans being clanked together.

"Mah, mah," she said, her dual accents tripping over each other, "ah seem to have taken a rawther long nap. Is there any coffee left?"

"Sure, honey." Nick sprang to her side with a cup. "Now you just relax. We've got everything under control." He turned to me. "Ann," he said, "you set the table. The silverware's in the drawer. The place mats are here, and the plates and glasses are in the cupboard."

One would have thought I was bucking for promotion the way I snapped to attention and bustled about performing my designated chores. Finally all was ready. Donnie, who'd spent an hour screaming, "I get to light the candles," climbed up on the table, knelt on his father's plate, and did so. Then we all sat down.

"Isn't this fun?" a revived Connie said as she lifted her wine glass in a toast. "We'll have to do it again next year."

I took a large gulp of wine and Joe coughed nervously.

"All right now, everyone," Nick proclaimed in his magician's voice, "pay attention. We're going to carve the bird." He waved the carving knife and bowed. Then he grabbed the leg and sliced.

117

At the first puncture, blood oozed out and ran down the side.

"Oooo, yuck," Chris squealed.

I looked at Joe. He was swallowing hard.

Connie winced. Then with a shake of her head she absolved herself. "I don't know how that could have happened," she said. "Nick, did you turn the oven down while I was asleep?"

"No." He stood with his knife still poised in the air like a conductor waiting for the downbeat.

"Well, someone must have done something." She shot me an accusatory glance and got up to check the oven. But the evidence was gone. The oven was off.

Nick waggled his head back and forth in disbelief. "Come on, honey," he said finally. "Sit down. We'll simply slice off the done parts, and then we'll put it back in to cook some more."

It wasn't an easy task. Even the white meat had a vibrant pink tinge to it. Suddenly appetites waned and there was a rush for cranberry sauce and gravy in the vain attempt to cover up the nearly raw meat. I helped myself to some salad and slid a lettuce leaf over some of my turkey.

When everyone had been served and it was obvious seconds wouldn't be in great demand, Connie put the bird back in the pan and in the oven.

"I still don't know how that happened," she mumbled.

I knew how it had happened, but silence seemed the better part of valor, so I concentrated on my potatoes. Everyone else did too, and within minutes all plates were bare.

"Anyone for more?" Nick thundered in a futile attempt to lighten the mood.

"No thanks."

"How about some salad?"

"Not for me."

"Potatoes?"

" 'Fraid not."

"Well then, why don't we clear all this away and have a little dessert?"

I stared at Joe, trying to bore into his mind the message that it was time to flee the scene of the disaster. I needn't have bothered. He'd thought of it himself.

"I tell you, Nick," he said, trying to look full, "I don't think I could eat another bite. In fact," he added, looking at his watch, "I think it's about time Ann and I wended our weary way home."

"So soon?" Connie trilled, and I tried to remember back to morning, at least a week before. "I thought we'd mix up another batch of drinks, and—"

"I'd sure like to"—Joe leapt in before she could go further—"but it's getting kind of late, and don't forget, tomorrow's a work day."

"Oh, stay," she insisted. "Maybe later, if we get hungry, we can have some turkey sandwiches."

That did it. I edged my way around her and scurried down the hall to the bedroom to get our coats. By the time I brought them back, Joe had the Mah-Jongg set under his arm and his hand firmly on the doorknob. It took a few more "no really's", and "we'd love to, but's" before we managed to get out the door and safely into the car.

"Whew," Joe said as we sped back across town, "I thought we'd never escape."

"I know." I stared out into the darkness. "What's more, we left them with half a bottle of gin, all those rotten leftovers we were supposed to share, and all three pies."

Joe slowed down. "Even the mince?" he wailed. "But that's my favorite."

"I know, I know," I said. "But I'm sure they'll come by tomorrow and bring it and the gin and whatever was our part of the turkey. That is if it ever finished cooking."

I knew not whereof I spoke. For though Nick did bring the mince pie, he didn't bring it to our house. Instead he included it, one piece at a time, in his lunch. And for once Joe broke his silence about goings-on at the office. I didn't even have to say, "How did things go today?"

Every day for a week, the minute he stepped inside the front door, he'd say, "Well, he did it again. He brought my pie in his lunchbox. He even had the audacity to tell me how good it was, and how well it went with his turkey sandwich."

I fanned the conversational flame with "He didn't!" "Oh, Joe, how could he?" "Tell me more."

Now that I think of it, it was almost worth it.

☆ ★ ☆ **12** ☆ ★ ☆

WHO'S NERVOUS?
NOT I

"The days dwindle down," as they say, "to a precious few." Unfortunately, as winter moved into what would, anyplace else, have been spring, I, unlike the days, did not dwindle. I expanded. I preceded myself into every room. I walked with the ungainly gait of someone tottering around carrying a week's worth of groceries. I also avoided lawn chairs and overstuffed sofas lest I have to be extricated from them mechanically.

At work my desk and I moved farther and farther apart. I had to stretch to reach the typewriter keys. And much of my time navigating around the office was spent bumping into things.

This made Tom, who rivaled Joe in anxiety, nervous. But then everything about my pregnancy made Tom nervous. All I had to do was yawn and he'd leap from his desk and rush into my office.

"Are you all right?"

"Sure, why?"

"I thought I heard you groan."

"Oh, come now, Tom. You're overreacting."

"I'm not. What if you give birth right here?"

"Good Lord, I'm not due till the middle of May."

"I know, but Mandy, the waitress in the coffee shop, said everyone in the building is laying bets on whether or not you deliver in the lobby."

"That's dumb. I know I may look a bit clumsy, lumbering even, but Dr. Bates has assured me I'm not going to deliver in the rice paddies, so to speak. And since I'm leaving soon, there's little chance you're going to have to boil water or rip sheets."

Tom did not like to be reminded that I was leaving. Not that he found me irreplaceable. It had taken him approximately ten minutes to come up with the idea of having Marge replace me. Five more minutes and he'd resolved the conflict of an orchestra member being the secretary. And another ten to get Marge to agree. There was one provision. On concert days I'd come down and man the box office, since Marge could hardly be expected to sell tickets till the last minute, then gallop down the center aisle with her cello tucked under her arm.

No, Tom wasn't averse to my leaving because he'd miss me. He simply didn't like change. More important, he was terrified I'd be rushed to the hospital before my April 18 retirement date, which would leave him explaining the inner workings of the office himself. And even he was aware he hadn't paid enough attention to know what they were.

So he panicked the day my collapsing chair did so as I reached toward the pencil sharpener, and I landed in an elephantine heap on the floor. He got jittery if I was late coming back from a doctor's appointment. And he almost drove out to the base to check on my safety the day the tornado hit Wichita Falls.

He needn't have worried. Even though it roared through shortly after I'd left for home, I was no slouch at beating the rush hour traffic. So when it hit I was in our front yard taking movies.

It was my first tornado, and one more than I'd expected to see. I'd been led to believe that an old Indian legend stating that tornadoes never cross the Wichita River protected the area. Of course the storm may not have realized that the trickle of water meandering

121

through town was a river. I certainly had taken a while to learn that fact. Still, when I left the office and looked up at the skies growing ever darker, the word "tornado" sprang quickly to mind. I even mentioned it to the man in the parking lot, but he pooh-poohed it and dragged up the old Indian's name again. So since I'm one of those who prefer legends to facts, I drove home expecting little more than a spring thunderstorm.

It started to hail shortly after I got in the house. At first it was tiny pellets that bounced in the grass and off the pavement and sounded as if someone were throwing handfuls of rice against the window.

"Hey, look at that," Joe said, pointing to the sky to the south of us.

The clouds were dark, almost black. They churned and boiled like ashen suds in a giant washer. Near the horizon there was a band of light, and black wisps of clouds dipped into it and receded again. The temperature had dropped. The air was chilly, and soon the hail grew bigger.

"I'm going to get a piece to save," Joe said, dashing out the back door.

"Why?"

"I don't know." He brought a huge hunk back and stuffed it in our tiny freezer. "It's just interesting, that's all."

He stared out the back door again. "Holy cow. Look at the size of them now." He ran back out and retrieved another, and another, and another.

He had to stop when we ran out of freezer space. As it was, he'd already thrown out two packages of succotash and a soup bone to make room for his collection.

"Enough already," I told him as I loaded up the movie camera and watched the trailing clouds dip and disperse. Suddenly a funnel formed.

"Look, Joe, look," I shouted, running out in the yard to get a better shot. "It's a tornado."

"Come back here."

"Don't worry," I yelled, "it's not coming this way." I aimed the camera and pressed. "Come on out. It's fascinating."

He came, and together we stood watching as the tornado, like a malevolent finger, touched down, rose, and touched down again. We couldn't see where it struck, but I imagined houses exploding and chickens being tossed into the air only to be set down unharmed miles away.

My imagination, luckily, was worse than the actual event. A trailer park was damaged slightly, but that was all. Finally it dissipated and we went back inside, I to rescue the succotash and Joe to defend his hailstones.

The nightly news with John Daly was on in the living room. Suddenly he stopped.

"I have a bulletin," he said. "A tornado has just hit Wichita Falls, Texas, during the evening rush hour. As yet we have no details. Stay tuned for further updates."

"How about that?" I said. "We made the national news."

Joe snuck another hailstone into the freezer. "Not bad," he said. "Not bad at all."

Tom was late for work the next morning. He'd been up half the night trying to call home to let his parents know he was safe. Consequently he overslept.

"How'd you like the excitement?" I said when he finally came in. "That was something, wasn't it?"

He snarled.

"I think I got it on film too."

"You what?"

"I took movies of it, and if I had the right settings it should be pretty interesting."

"You mean you went outside—in your condition—with a tornado raging through the skies?"

"Sure, why not? It wasn't close to us."

He shook his head. "I'll sure feel better when you're safely out of this office."

"Oh, really. You're worse than Joe." I took him a cup of coffee. "Besides, Tom," I said, setting it down on his desk, "it's not going to be that long. Marge is coming in next week, and then before you know it I'll be gone."

I was too. After a traditional "see you later—it's been fun—we've passed the hat—and here's a gift" party, I cleaned out my desk, thanked Dr. Kohary for his patience, told Tom to get with it on his correspondence, wished Marge all sorts of good luck, and headed home to await motherhood.

Joe was delighted to have me back at my post. Vicar was ecstatic. The months of being locked inside the house or tied to the clothesline had not sat well with him. And he'd made his complaints known. This had not endeared him or us to weird Willard and the assortment of new neighbors who'd moved in in my absence.

Normally I would have had a chance to introduce him to them casually. I would have been able to point out his sterling qualities to them and let them appreciate his personality as an individual, as Joe and I did. But while I was working, there didn't seem to be time. Winter evenings were no occasion for strolling up and down the street saying, "How do you do? Have you met my eccentric dog?" And weekends were spent motoring behind the vacuum cleaner or standing at the washing machine.

For a while Marge had acted as an intermediary. But then the government in a whimsical mood decided to discontinue charging rent in favor of snatching the entire housing allowance. So she and Ted moved out and took an inexpensive apartment in town. And Vicar was left howling at the clothesline alone.

Ruth and Stan Rieban, the people who moved in, were probably the least charmed by Vicar's mournful cry. They presented their grievances shortly after I returned to housewife status, or rather Ruth did. She was specific. She was also emphatic, and while I was the essence of remorse and contrition while she presented her case, by the time Joe came home for lunch, I was ranting.

"What are we going to do?" I said as I wandered around the kitchen slapping his sandwich together and getting him some soup. "She says Vicar's barking brought on a miscarriage, and that if we don't do something, and now, she's going to call the Air Police."

"Don't get so upset," he said. "You're home now, and he won't be tied up so often. So the whole problem should simply disappear."

I wasn't about to be consoled. I ranted on and on, enumerating the tragedies obviously in store. Joe trailed after me with a bewildered "Who let in the maniac?" look on his face.

Poor Joe. He'd expected midnight demands for pickles and ice cream. He was also prepared for some emotionalism. But I'd exceeded all bounds of his imagination.

One minute I, like a reincarnation of Suzy Homemaker, was waxing floors, scrubbing shelves, and ironing clothes that hadn't seen daylight in eight months. I was the soul of efficiency, making my infamous lists and crossing off the completed tasks with military precision. The next thing he knew I was in tears because Mother had sent me a book on baby care.

"But honey," he'd say, putting his arm around my shoulder but trying to keep his uniform dry, "I don't understand. I thought you were thrilled with the book."

"I was," I'd sob. "But then I read it."

"What did it say that has you so upset?"

"Everything. Here, for instance"—and I'd flip through to the section on baby's toys— "it says, 'When baby's rattle is thrown from the crib or baby's playpen it should not be returned to him unless it has first been washed with soap, rinsed thoroughly, and boiled for five minutes.' How am I going to be able to get anything done if I have to spend all my time boiling toys?"

"Oh, sweetheart, don't worry. I don't think we have to be that antiseptic."

"But it says here—"

"Never mind what it says. Now put the book away and cheer up."

So, flipping moods again like a professional flapjack turner, I'd cheer up, and we'd have dinner and laugh about whether or not we were going to have to boil Vicar. After the dishes were done and the kitchen was cleaned, we'd work for a while refinishing the secondhand nursery furniture we'd bought. Then we'd go to bed, and I could almost hear Joe heave a sigh of relief that he'd made it through another day.

He was right to be apprehensive. For though he might come home after work the next night and find the table set, dinner bubbling on the stove, and fresh bread in the oven, he also might walk in to find me snarling and spitting because the spaghetti sauce had burned or the rice was gummy.

As a rule he was patient and consoling. But every now and then even he could stand it no more.

"Oh, stop acting like a child," he'd snap as I banged pots and pans around and slammed the cupboard doors.

And I, who at that point was thoroughly enjoying my misery, would rear back. "And what do you mean by that?"

"Just what I said. Stop acting like a child. In short, grow up."

"Well," I'd huff. Then because I knew he was right, but wasn't about to admit it, I'd search back to the day we met and list, from that time forward, in chronological order, every instance where he'd acted less than mature.

He rarely stayed for the entire inventory. He either stomped into the living room and sat down to read the paper or else went into the bedroom and shut the door.

One night even that didn't suffice. When I launched into the body of my harangue, he held up his hand.

"That's it," he said. "I'm not about to stick around and listen to any more of this. Goodbye."

With that he grabbed the car keys from the counter and slammed out the front door. Normally I would have sputtered for a while, then simmered, and finally cooled off. But what prospective mother ever acts normal?

As soon as I heard the car start, I rushed to the phone. I could hardly dial fast enough, and when Mother—at home, unsuspecting, and unprepared—answered, I burst into racking sobs.

"Mo—O—ther," I howled, "Jo—O—e's left me."

"Joe's what?"

"He's left me."

"Now wait a minute. Calm down. I can't understand you. You say Joe has left you?"

"Yes. We had this huge fight, and, and, he just walked out the door and left me."

"When?"

"A few minutes ago."

There was a pause. "Now honey," she said, sounding much calmer than I liked, "he probably just wanted to be by himself for a while. He'll be back."

"No he won't. He's left me for good, forever. Here I am about to give birth to a baby that's going to have to grow up without a father."

There was a silence, and I thought I heard muffled laughter, but decided it must be the phone connection. Finally Mother spoke. "Now Annie," she said, "I know you're upset, but I'm sure there's nothing to worry about. Go wash your face with cold water, and—"

"Wait a minute," I broke in. "I think I hear him coming back. Goodbye." I hung up.

Needless to say, Joe was more than amazed when, as he stalked in the door, I rushed over and threw my arms around him.

"You've come back," I gushed. "You've actually come back. Forgive me. I promise I'll never be mean and rotten again."

I doubt he believed me. I doubt I believed me. I've certainly never refrained from being mean and rotten since then. But at the time, it seemed to be a wonderful healing thing to say.

Luckily, as my delivery date got closer, I got calmer. Joe, on the other hand, started to fidget and bite his nails. He took to calling home three and four times a day. If I was outside and had to run to answer the phone and was out of breath when I said hello, he thought I was in labor.

"I'll be right home," he'd shout, and it was all I could do to explain. "No, no, I was simply running."

"But you shouldn't be running."

"Don't worry. I'm fine."

"Oh, all right, but you call me if anything happens, even if I'm in class."

This proved he was nervous. Interrupting class was almost a treasonable offense.

He was even worse at home. Sometimes when I got up in the middle of the night, I'd come back to bed and find him sitting bolt upright.

"Is it time?" he'd say, grabbing for his clothes.

"No, it's not time. Go back to sleep."

Then one evening it was time.

"Oh, my God," Joe said when I apprised him of the situation. "Now what do we do?"

"Call Dr. Bates first, I guess." I looked at my watch. It was ten-thirty. "I hope he's not already in bed."

"What do you mean you hope he's not already in bed?" he snapped. "Do you propose to wait till he gets up?"

"No. It was a dumb statement."

"What's his number?"

"It's by the phone."

It took two tries to get him. The first number Joe dialed turned out to be a loading dock somewhere in town. Because he ranted on about deliveries and time of arrival it was a while before the conversation unraveled itself and he realized his mistake.

Finally he reached Dr. Bates. I couldn't tell much from the conversation, but at last he hung up.

"What'd he say?"

"He said wait till the pains are five minutes apart. Then call the hospital and tell them we're on our way. They will let him know."

"Great," I said. "Now what do we do in the meantime, play cribbage?"

"Clever." He started for the kitchen, changed his mind, headed into the bedroom, changed his mind again, then simply stood there. Then he snapped his fingers. "Are you packed?"

I made a face. "No. I was scared to. I figured if I was all ready it would make the baby late."

"OK, then we'll pack. Where's the suitcase?"

"In the other room. Here I'll get it."

"No, you sit on the bed. I'll get it."

"Can't I make myself some more coffee first?"

"No."

So I sat on the bed and directed the proceedings, and when Joe had packed everything but my raincoat and a bathing suit, we sat and stared at each other.

"Shouldn't we be going?" he asked, his passion for promptness coming to the fore.

"No. It's still eight minutes between pains."

"Oh." He fidgeted with the paper, straightening the pages and arranging the sections. Then he took my cup into the kitchen. Then he went outside and emptied the garbage.

Finally it was time to go. I went out to the car while Joe called the hospital.

"I want you to keep calm," he said as we drove up the block and circled back. "They said not to rush. We have plenty of time."

"I'm calm," I assured him.

As we approached the gate I could see the guard. He looked lonely standing there all by himself in his little telephone booth hut. When we drove up he stepped out, squinted as he checked our bumper sticker, and waved us on.

All of a sudden Joe swerved and pulled over to the side of the road.

"What are you doing?" I said. "He told us to go on."

"He didn't salute," he snapped. Then before I could stop him, he was out of the car and headed back to the gate.

"What's your name, Airman?" I heard him bark as I cringed in my seat and noted the pains were now four minutes apart.

"Lummus, sir. Matthew Lummus."

"Well, Airman Lummus, is it your usual practice not to salute an officer when he drives through?"

"No, sir."

"Or did you decide it was late and you were perhaps a little tired?"

"No, sir."

"When I drive through I expect to be saluted."

"Yes, sir."

"Even when I'm not in uniform."

"Yes, sir."

"All right. I'll overlook it this once."

"Thank you, sir."

"Good night, Airman Lummus."

"Yes, sir. Thank you, sir. Good night, sir."

I turned around. The poor boy was ramrod straight and saluting as if his life were in danger. Joe returned the salute, marched back to the car and got in. I kept quiet. I thought it was wise.

Then, as we headed on down the road, he turned to me. "Why did I do that?" he asked.

"Who knows." I laughed. "But I bet that poor devil never forgets to salute again."

Joe grimaced. "Probably not."

I patted his arm. "Don't worry," I said. "He's heard worse. Now step on it. The pains are three minutes apart."

"Oh, my Lord," he gasped, and the car lurched ahead.

Two and a half hours later, at 2:28 A.M., David Michael Combs came into the world, and he didn't even salute.

☆ ★ ☆ 13 ☆ ★ ☆

$E=mc^2$

Albert Einstein was right. Everything is relative. And to prove his theory one need only add to one's life—a relative. A small, round, hungry, constantly damp relative.

Suddenly laundry, heretofore a casual part of a Monday morning or a Wednesday afternoon, expands to become a full-time occupation. Night, previously eight or more hours of darkness strung together for the purpose of rest and sleep, becomes a series of short naps punctuated with feedings, which in themselves seem to last for eight or more hours. And a house, once so large you had to shout to anyone absent-mindedly listening in the next room, suddenly shrinks, and even a whimper behind a closed door sounds like a Tarzan yell, and jolts you out of the deepest slumber.

During the daylight hours I was the perfect mother. I fed David. I bathed him and changed him with a lilt in my voice and a song in my heart. I gurgled and cooed. I made faces and told stories. I discussed current events, commented on the weather, and asked for advice on different baby powders. I washed diapers, and more diapers, and more diapers. I rinsed them and rushed them out to the clothesline, where, like a battalion of white flags surrendering, they waved and whipped in the wind.

I rocked. I sang lullabies. And when I ran out of lullabies I included a few verses of "Lloyd George Knew My Father" and "The Maine Stein Song" for variety.

During the daylight hours Joe was the perfect father. He took his turn at the changing table. He hung out laundry and gathered it in again. He held David and sat in the rocker explaining which was Huntley and which was Brinkley, while I warmed the bottle and cooked dinner. And when the spray truck, the base's answer to mosquito netting, stopped in the schoolyard behind our house so the driver could have a smoke, Joe raced outside, waved his arms, fired an expletive or two, and urged them to move on.

Then came night. After the dishes had been done. After the mountain of diapers had been folded and we'd watched the late news. After we'd tucked David into bed after his final evening feeding, the perfect parents retired to bed.

Imperfection began somewhere around one-thirty or two with the first sounds of complaint and hunger from the nursery.

It didn't show up right away. For the first two or three nights I leapt up as soon as I heard murmuring.

"Go back to sleep," Joe would say as he too rolled out of bed. "I'll take this one."

"No, no," I'd insist. "You have to go to work in the morning. You need your rest. I'll get it."

Then I'd bound into the kitchen, put a bottle on to warm, and rush in to quiet David so Joe could go back to sleep. The process was simple. I'd change and feed and change again. I'd rock and sing and pat his back. And when every need had been taken care of I'd put him back to bed and watch in delight as his head popped up again. Then Joe, who couldn't stand missing the excitement, would wander in and pat him and rock the crib till he went back to sleep. Then we'd both tiptoe back to our own bed, and after a brief discussion about what a marvelous child we had we too would sleep.

Then things started to change. I first noticed it the night I woke up with David already at full bellow.

"Joe?" I said, poking the inert figure lying beside me. "Honey?

131

Do you think you could take this shift? I wouldn't ask, but I'm exhausted."

"Huh?" he said, and then he mumbled something else and pulled the sheet up over his ears.

"Joe?" I said again. "Sweetheart?" I shook his shoulder. "Could you feed David this time? I'm so tired, I don't think I'll be able to stay awake. Please?"

He turned over. "I tell you what," he said, sounding strangely alert, "I'll pick a number between one and ten, and if you guess it, I'll feed David."

"Oh, all right." I thought a moment. "How about six?"

"Wrong, you lose." And he turned back on his side. "See you later."

"Oh, OK." I struggled out of bed and stumbled off into the kitchen. Because I am not swift, even when wide awake and rested, it wasn't till half an hour later, when I was slumped in the rocking chair watching David finish off the last of his milk, that I realized I'd been had.

Of course I didn't fall for that trick again. But then Joe didn't try it again either. He had others.

"I was just up with him half an hour ago," he'd say, knowing full well I'd be too groggy to doubt his word.

"I have an important briefing in the morning, and I have to be alert."

"I'll take the next one."

I didn't give up though. Sometimes when I happened to hear the first stirrings and knew a roar was due at any minute, I kicked Joe. Not hard, just enough to wake him up. Then I lay perfectly still and tried to outlast him.

At times even my subconscious took pity on me. I dreamt that someone else was standing by my bed saying, "Now, now, Ann. You stay right where you are. I'm going to attend to that young man in there."

Once it was even David Brinkley. Of course he was more formal about it. But still, as I woke up, he was just telling me not to worry about his missing a newscast. "Your sleep is more important."

It wasn't that those late night feedings actually took so long. They only seemed to. From the time I dragged into the kitchen, pounding on the walls as I went so the Texas cockroaches that skitter around at night would disappear, till at last I crept back into my own bed, it felt as if days had passed.

The watched pot that never boils sat on the stove, stared back at me as I willed it to hurry, and never boiled. The midnight darkness tapped at the windows and reminded me the rest of the world was asleep. And in our room I could hear Joe snoring and almost feel how comfortable he must be, horizontal, relaxed, unconscious.

There were no Late Late Shows to take my mind off the fact that at best it would be forty-five minutes till I'd be able to crawl back into bed. No youthful Robert Young made me forget that even at this hour it was hot, and my back was sticking to the chair. Even the radio stations signed off at midnight. And though Vicar greeted me when David and I first ventured out, soon he too stretched out on the floor and went to sleep.

So there we sat. Every now and then I heard a car drive past the house, and sometimes I amused myself by listening to planes landing on the runway to the east. But for the most part, I struggled to keep awake, and wondered if perhaps I was in a time warp that would go on forever.

Marge assured me it would end.

"It's got to," she told me one day when I called the symphony and, because Tom was out playing golf, she was able to talk. "Ted says all babies sleep through the night by the time they're three months old."

"Perhaps," I sighed, "but by then I will have aged ten years."

"Why don't you take a nap when he's sleeping in the afternoon?"

"I would, but I've always been led to believe there's something evil about naps."

"Oh, don't be silly." Suddenly her voice changed and I could tell that Tom was back. "I'll send those tickets out to you right away," she said.

"I'll talk to you later." And we both hung up.

I eyed the bed, sitting there all prim and proper with its sheets tucked in securely and its spread ruffling in the wind from the air cooler.

Maybe, just this once, I thought. After all, David isn't due to wake up for another hour yet. I remembered the lunch dishes still sitting in the sink. So what, I argued with myself. I'll still have plenty of time to do them before Joe gets home.

I sat down on the edge, just to test. It was soft. I lay down and closed my eyes. Every bone in my body unhinged, and I wondered briefly how it was possible to be so completely comfortable.

Suddenly the phone rang. I jumped up like a little girl caught trying on her mother's jewelry and stumbled in to answer before it woke David.

"Hello?"

"Hi, honey." Joe sounded disgustingly cheerful and rested. "I just called to see how you were."

"Me?" I stifled a yawn. "Oh, I'm fine, just fine. In fact," I lied, "I was headed outside. I have to bring in the laundry before David wakes up."

"Oh, good." Nothing pleased Joe more than the troops keeping gainfully employed in his absence. "Well, then I'll let you go."

He hung up, and because guilt is my co-pilot, I rejected any further attempts at a nap and got back to work.

"I might as well get used to this," I grumbled to myself as I dried the last of the dishes. " 'Cause it looks as if it will be this way forever."

That night, however, when at the ten o'clock feeding David gobbled down his milk and cried for more, I felt a flicker of hope in my exhausted soul.

"I think he's stoking up for the night," I told Joe. "What do you bet he sleeps clear through?"

"He probably will."

He didn't. What went down came right back up again, so we had to start all over again. The same thing happened the next morning, and again at noon.

When Joe walked in the door at noon, I was on the phone to Dr. Sullivan.

"What'd he say?" he asked when I hung up.

"He said dilute the formula. He thinks it might be too rich."

"Oh." Joe was watching me closely. "And what do you think?"

"What do you mean?"

"Well, you look as if you don't agree with the good doctor."

"Oh, I do. It's just that—"

"That what?"

"Well, I looked the symptoms up in Dr. Spock."

"That's not the boil-everything book, is it?"

"No, no. That's another one. Anyway, as I said, I looked up the symptoms, and it sounds to me as if David has pyloric stenosis."

"What?" Joe was skeptical at best. "What do you mean?"

"Look here." I showed him the book. "See, 'projectile vomiting shortly after feeding . . . common in boy babies . . . usually occurs in three weeks.' It all fits."

"Now Annie"—Joe handed back the book—"don't you think if it were—whatever it is you called it—that Dr. Sullivan would know?"

"Yes, I guess so. Still—"

"Still nothing. Dilute the formula just as he said. Then if that doesn't help, you can tell him you think it's this other thing."

"Oh, all right."

But my resolve faltered in the afternoon. And at the risk of being labeled a hysterical new mother, I called Dr. Sullivan again.

"You see," I explained when he came on the phone, "it's just that all the symptoms fit, and I think he's losing weight, and he seems so pathetic, and, and, . . ." I tried to keep my voice steady and reasonable. I failed.

"Now Ann," he said in that wonderful voice doctors have that's reminiscent of cavalry hooves thundering over the ridge, "I know it sounds similar, but believe me, I doubt it. However," he added when my snuffling and hiccuping led him to believe I wasn't convinced, "if it will make you feel better, why don't you bring him down and I'll take a look."

Two days later Joe and I sat in David's hospital room waiting for them to bring him back from surgery.

David went through the operation beautifully. I thought I did too. I limited myself to only a couple of emotional phone calls home to Mother. I was the epitome of cool and calm when they took him off to surgery. And I refrained from weeping when they

135

brought him back and he looked so pale and still.

Then because I was allowed to stay in his room with him, I met the night nurse.

She was young, about twenty, but her dedication and devotion to rules seemed to have been around, hardening, for years. The trouble started with the weigh-in. She'd been given instructions to weigh the patient before and after each feeding, and she was determined to do just that, by herself, and without interference.

"It's the rules," she told me the first night when she popped in half an hour after he'd finished and found, to her obvious horror, that I had changed his clothes. "The patient is to be weighed both times in the same clothing."

"But he was wet."

"Exactly, and that wetness should be included in his final weight."

"So why don't I weigh him if you're not here?"

She recoiled. "I couldn't do that. Hospital regulations require a trained nurse to perform such duties."

"That's stupid," I blurted. "What's so mystical about weighing a baby?"

"Mrs. Combs," she said, fixing me with the stony stare of someone who owns the game, has memorized the rules, and will tolerate no exceptions, "you are not trained. I am. Now if you will please hand me the wet diaper in the pail over there, I will try to undo the damage you have done."

I did so. Then I sat back and watched as she weighed first a dry diaper, and then the wet one. She scribbled on a pad, figured out the difference and added it to David's total weight.

"How about his undershirt?" I asked, not about to make her job easier. "I changed that too, and it was damp."

She sighed. Obviously it wasn't easy mingling with the ignorant. "Why didn't you mention that before?"

I shrugged. "I forgot," I said.

She didn't believe me. "Is this the shirt you changed?" she said, rummaging around in the diaper pail.

"That's it." I waited as she went through the weighing process again. Then, because this was beginning to be fun, I added, "Did you account for the evaporation too? After all it's been in there at least an hour, and what with the air conditioning going full blast and all . . ."

She whipped around. "This is a hospital, Mrs. Combs," she snapped. "It is not—"

A knock on the door interrupted her intended harangue, and before I could answer, Dr. Sullivan walked in.

"Well, well," he said, "and how is everyone this fine night? How are you, Miss Benson?"

She glared at him. "Everything is fine, Dr. Sullivan," she said, "when I'm not hampered in the performance of my duties. Now if you will excuse me." And she was gone.

"What was that all about?" he asked.

"Oh, nothing. She was just mad because I changed David's diapers, and she had to weigh them."

"She what?"

I explained.

"Oh, Lord," he groaned, "save me from efficient nurses. From now on, tell Miss Benson that I have given you orders to change diapers whenever you see fit."

"Oh, I will. I will," I chortled. "I can hardly wait."

Unfortunately I had to. Miss Benson was off duty the next night, and after that we took David home.

Dr. Sullivan came by before we left. "All right," he said as I packed up the last of his clothes. "Now I want you to remember that though the operation was a complete success, David may spit up once or twice in the next day or two. But it's nothing to worry about, and he'll be fine after that."

He was too. When we got him home it was as if there had never been any trouble. He ate and slept. He cooed and crowed. And every once in a while, when he'd eaten sumptuously at the late evening meal, he slept through till five or six.

I wallowed in the luxury of uninterrupted rest, and though I was present and accounted for at all sunrises, I didn't complain. It was enough to know I'd missed the underbelly of the night session.

Then one night in June he slept through at ten.

I panicked. "Should we wake him?" I asked Joe, who was watching the late news.

"Huh?"

"Should we wake David and feed him now to keep him from getting up in an hour or two?"

"No, let him sleep."

"But, I'd rather get it over with now."

"Then wake him."

"But what if he's going to go clear through till morning?"

"Then don't."

Joe's no help when I'm trying to foist a decision on him, so I can blame him later if things go wrong. Finally, cowardice and a selfish longing for another full night of slumber took over. I woke David up and forced eight ounces of nutrition down him. The next night I did the same thing, and the next, and the next.

Summer wore on and in August I took him in to Dr. Sullivan for a three-month check-up. Dr. Sullivan was amazed at his progress.

"Good God," he said, "what have you been feeding this child?"

"What do you mean?"

"He's gained six pounds since I last saw him."

"But—but," I stammered, searching for a reason, "he only eats three meals a day, and then of course I wake him at ten—"

"You what?"

"I wake him at ten."

"Why on earth would you do that?"

"Well . . ." I drawled, sensing I was in deep trouble, "if I don't he'll wake up in the middle of the night."

"Are you serious?"

"Of course."

He shook his head, "Oh, Ann, Ann, Ann," he said, as if to a four-year-old, "take my word for it. That boy is not about to wake up from hunger in the middle of the night."

"But."

"No buts. I'm ordering you to cut out the ten o'clock feedings."

"Oh, all right, but if he does, I'm going to call you right away and tell you about it."

"It's a deal."

I wavered that night, around eleven.

"Do you think he'll really sleep through?" I asked Joe.

"Sure."

"But what if he doesn't?"

"Good grief. If he doesn't, he doesn't. Now shut up and come to bed."

So I wrapped my cloak of doubts tightly around me, tiptoed in for one last look and went to bed.

The next morning at eight-thirty, after Joe had left for work, after I'd had breakfast and read the paper, after I'd put in a load of wash, and had checked three times to be sure he was still alive, David woke up. I rushed in to bid him a rested good morning.

"Well, love," I said as I lifted him out of the crib, "Mr. Einstein will be glad to know. The universe has settled back into place."

David cooed and pulled at my hair. He'd known all along. This time warp was only temporary.

☆ ★ ☆ **14** ☆ ★ ☆

YOU'RE GOING WHERE?
FOR HOW LONG?

Officially TDY is temporary duty. It's a week or ten days or six months when the Air Force husband is sent off by quadruplicate orders to tour bases in Greenland or attend briefings in California or inspect facilities in Guam.

Unofficially it's a week or ten days or six months when the Air Force wife learns to fend for herself, to pay the bills and retrieve the cleaning, and have the transmission fixed. It's when she takes up bowling, enrolls in a sewing class, cleans out the closets, rearranges all the furniture, subsists on scrambled eggs and TV dinners, reads novels late into the night, works on jigsaw puzzles, writes letters to almost anyone, goes to office parties alone, and comes home early.

Traditionally it's also the time when the washing machine breaks, and the repairman can't come till next week. It's when the dog bites the mailman, when the water heater explodes in the middle of the night, when the children get high fevers and mysterious rashes, when the fan belt breaks, when the oven catches fire, and when

140

the bank makes an error and sends a week's worth of checks back stamped NSF.

TDY comes to everyone eventually. And after a long hot summer, a long hot fall, a Thanksgiving without the Gibbs and with mince pie; after David's first Christmas, followed by a quiet New Year's Eve with Napa valley champagne and a Guy Lombardo waltz or two, TDY came to us. On the eighth of January Joe packed up his uniforms and his suitcase and left for three months in Montgomery, Alabama, at Squadron Officers School.

He also left me dusting off my blue brocade again and wondering if we weren't carrying this parenthood thing a bit far and a bit fast. I didn't have much chance for complaint though. It's considered bad form to burden the hero while he's away conquering missile systems and strike force potentials. And with Marge and Ted's move into town and Vicar's dubious success at public relations, there weren't a lot of sympathetic ears in the neighborhood waiting for my lamentations about pregnancy and TDY.

Luckily David was amenable to any and all conversation. In the morning we discussed oatmeal and its proper place in the mouth rather than through the hair. We debated the question of simple bathing versus whacking the water to see how far it will shoot. We entertained the idea of indulging in yet another teething biscuit before lunch. And we mentioned that neatness counts, and though it's exhilarating to throw a can of powder to the floor it's also messy.

In the afternoon after David had rested from a busy morning of emptying the cupboards and rolling tomato sauce cans across the floor, we headed out to the commissary or the BX to do errands. Then we came back, and while he joined his stuffed animals in the playpen and reported to them on his day's activities, I got dinner.

Evenings we sat in the rocker and read or watched TV. *The Noisy Books* were a great favorite. They detailed the adventures of a small black dog named Muffin who for some reason or other couldn't see and had to listen to all the sounds around him. I soon became an expert at imitating everything from frogs to interurban buses screeching to a stop.

On Wednesdays we put the books away and watched *Wagon Train*. David loved Wednesdays. I neighed and mooed at the appropriate times. David giggled and flailed about, and Ward Bond yelled, "Wagons, ho."

Then David retired, and I occupied myself with diaper folding, dishwashing, and an occasional long hot bath. It was an easygoing life, but I missed Joe, especially in the evenings.

Then one night in mid-January, shortly after I'd settled David down, there was a knock at my back door. Ruth Rieban had come on a peace mission. Apparently she felt the dust had settled with any pre-, post-, or intra-natal jitters, and it was now safe to offer a gesture of friendship. She was right. I was delighted to see her. In fact I'd even considered loading the peace pipe myself. For though I enjoy a feud as much as the next person, and though I have relatives who carry grudges like saddlebags for so long they forget why, I had to admit I was a bit lonely and would enjoy conversations that were less one-sided and more syllabic.

Of course I did talk to Marge every now and then, but our phone calls were usually abbreviated, especially if Tom was in the office. But for the most part David and I were by ourselves. The Gibbs had been reassigned to Ellsworth Air Force Base in South Dakota. Jan Epler had taken a job as a substitute teacher, and the rest of the women connected with the office were busy with their own lives.

So while David was great company, and was especially witty at bedtime, I enjoyed having someone next door to have coffee with, and it was a treat to hear about something more complicated than a wet diaper. Besides, once I got to know her, Ruth let me hide in her house whenever I saw the Hescocks headed my way.

I'd met the Hescocks at church shortly after Joe and I moved out to the base. Getting to know them was unavoidable, for Episcopal services in the Air Force do not draw crowds. At Sheppard they barely drew the famous "two or three gathered together." It may have been because they were scheduled at seven on Sunday mornings. It was the only time not already reserved by the Catholics, the Lutherans, the Methodists, the Congregationalists, the General Conference Baptists, the Independent Baptists, the Conservative Baptists, the Southern Baptists, and the Regular Baptists. It may also have been because they were held in what could easily have passed for a converted coat closet.

Whatever the reason, the congregation as a rule consisted of Joe and me, the Hescocks, Chaplain Wickham and his wife, Mildred, who as a loyal clergy spouse always sat in the front pew, boomed out the "amens," and came equipped with a surplus of cough drops and Kleenex. Every once in a while a young airman and his tiny wife showed up, and a couple of times I saw a burly sergeant who came late, sat in the back, and left before the service was over. But that was about all.

Don and Barb Hescock had three children: Mandy who was eight, Josh six and a half, and Pam four. They were sweet children—blond, blue-eyed, and painfully shy. Most of the time they sat like statues. But every once in a while Mandy would get bored, give Josh a poke, and get a poke in return. This resulted in swift and certain censure, so it wasn't a frequent occurrence.

When Joe and I first met them they were more than gracious, and when they invited us over for an evening of dessert and bridge we accepted with pleasure. The pleasure vanished almost immediately, for though they were obviously a devoted couple, the glue that seemed to hold them together was the fact they both loved insulting each other.

"I bid three clubs, Horseface," Don would say, fanning out his cards.

"Three clubs, eh," Barb would answer. "OK, Mule Breath, I'll raise you to four."

"Four no-trump, Lard Legs."

"Five hearts, Four Eyes."

Once they got to know us, they included us in their repertoire.

"Is it your bid, Welterweight?" Barb would ask me.

"No, Stupid," Don would say, "it's Onion Head's bid."

Needless to say, about this time our attendance at church dropped off dramatically. Of course it didn't do much good. They sought us out, and when toward the end of January they found out Joe had gone on TDY, they made it a family project to keep me out of trouble and occupied.

During the week Barb would drop by in the afternoon with a week's worth of ironing to keep her hands busy while she visited.

"Thought you might like a little company," she'd holler as she barged in the door. "Now get out that crappy excuse for an iron, and put on some of your godawful coffee. I have to get Don's shitty shirts ironed, or he'll kill me for sure."

On Sundays they came after church, somewhere between seven forty-five and eight.

"Lookee what I've got here, you hideous heathen you," Don would say, thrusting a package of sweet rolls at me. "Now heat 'em up and get out some plates and silverware, and we'll have ourselves a breakfast."

Because I have no strength of character I usually did as I was told, and while I made juice and got the butter, they sat down and destroyed the Sunday paper.

I'd never seen anything like it. By the time they were through, it looked as if we'd been house training a brace of St. Bernards. Pages were scattered all over the room. Stories begun on A1 were forever separated from their endings on A7. And what pages were left in sequence were all but folded, stapled, and mutilated.

The first couple of times they came for a Sunday visit, I assumed they'd left the children at home. I was wrong. They were out in the car. They'd been told, "Stay there and shut up. We'll be back in a while."

Naturally when I learned they were out there I insisted they be allowed to come in. This was a mistake. Now the visits, which heretofore had lasted two to two and a half hours, lengthened to four.

It was obvious, even to me, that I was going to have to do something if I wanted my life back. So because I'm mature, reasonable, intelligent, and self-possessed, the something I chose to do was to hide. During the week, if I had ample warning, I galloped over to Ruth's and cowered in her kitchen.

On Sundays I set my alarm for seven-thirty. Then at the first sound of a car pulling up in front, I leapt up and dashed into the shower, where as everyone knows it's impossible to hear the doorbell.

Invitations by phone were easier to handle, and by early March I'd become an accomplished liar.

"Oh, hi, Barb," I'd say, pausing for a racking cough just in case. "How about coming up to have dinner?"

"Gee, I'd love to, but I don't have a sitter for David."

"Bring Lump-lump along then."

"I would, but, but he has a cold, and a rash, and I have to fold laundry, and the dog's lost, and I'm painting a chair, and I already have dinner in the oven, and . . . and . . . my car's almost out of gas."

Sometimes I went on for hours, but the most effective excuse was that Joe was due to call any minute. For one thing it precluded my leaving home. For another it meant I had to hang up and leave the line free. And the fact that he only called on Fridays between eight and eight-thirty remained a secret.

I looked forward to Joe's calls all week, and by the time they came through I was waiting like a catalogue shopper with my list of things to order. I'd jotted down subjects all week. They were earth-shattering. David had a new tooth and was sitting up. Vicar had escaped twice and been brought home by the Air Police once. The car sounded funny. Marge and I had gone to see *The Fly* while Ted baby-sat. Tom and Dr. Kohary were attending some kind of convention, which left Marge alone in the office. The Riebans had a new car. And, "I wish you'd hurry up and come home."

Joe had his own list. But at times it was hard to hear it. He called from the officers' club, where he and some of his classmates went for dinner every Friday, and from the sound of the background noise they weren't the only ones. In fact I wouldn't have been surprised to hear that it was SOP for everyone on the base to assemble there each week for dinner and drinks, and more drinks, and two for the road.

One week I made the mistake of being out when he called. I didn't think he'd worry. David and I had gone into town to Marge and Ted's for dinner, and I assumed when I didn't answer the phone he'd guess as much and call the next night. I assumed wrong. The phone was ringing when I walked in the door at ten. I dumped David, still in his snowsuit, into his crib and ran to answer it.

"Hello?" I said.

There was heavy breathing on the other end of the line, and remembering rule number one for those receiving obscene phone calls, I started to hang up. Then I heard a deep sigh, and voice with a familiar ring to it said, "Shaywhereyoubeen?"

"Joe?"

"That'sright. It'smeyourlittleoldloverboyJoe."

The peculiar lilt in his voice told me he'd been too long at the grape.

"DidyouknowIbeencallingyouforhoursandhours?" He giggled idiotically. "Don'ttellmeyou'vebeenoutonadate."

I felt my jaw tighten. I was stone cold sober. My feet were wet. I still had to get David to bed, and from the way he was bouncing up and down in his crib, it looked as if it would take a while. And Vicar was at the back door whining to get out.

"No, Joe," I said in my schoolmarm settle-down-children voice. "David and I were having dinner at Marge's."

"That'snice," he drawled, making it a fifteen-syllable sentence. "That'sreallynice. DoyouknowhowmuchIloveyou?"

"Yes, Joe." At this point I didn't really care. "Now why don't you hang up and I'll talk to you next week."

"ButIwanttotalktoyounow. You'remybeeutifulbeeutifulwife."

"Sure, sure, and you're drunk."

"I'mnotdrunk. Ijustmissmybaby." He lowered his voice conspiratorily. "You'remybabyaren'tyou?" he said.

"Oh, Joe," I groaned, "say goodbye."

"Goodbye? WhyshouldIsaygoodbye? Thenightisyoung."

"Not here it isn't. The night's old and I'm getting old with it. Now I have to go put David to bed."

"Noyoudon't."

"I do. Goodbye." And I slammed the phone down so hard it bounced.

David thought it was funny. He stood in his crib gnawing on the railing. "Bang," he said. "Bang, bang." Then he laughed and jumped up and down.

"Bang yourself," I snarled. I unzipped his snowsuit, put on his pajamas, and gave him his bear. "Now you lie down and go to sleep."

Even after I'd taken a shower and was in my own bed, I could hear him in the other room hitting his slats, giggling, and saying, "Bang."

I was not amused. It seems to me, I told myself as I lay staring

146

at the ceiling, that if Joe only calls once a week, and I wait and wait for that one call, the least he could do is be sober. I then reviewed all the hardships I'd endured since he left. I wallowed in a little self-pity. I went back to righteous indignation. And finally, in the middle of a vow that I'd stay mad forever, I drifted off to sleep.

By the next day I'd cooled down somewhat. And on Sunday when Joe called again, to apologize, I even managed to regale him with a description of David vaulting up and down shouting "Bang" while I fumed and swore.

"I'm so sorry," he said.

"Oh, that's all right. I just wish it were April and you were on your way back."

"I do too, honey, but it won't be long now."

It was long though. The weeks dragged by. March stretched out like a Texas highway, on and on with no end in sight. Monday seemed to take three days to work its way into Tuesday, and weekends were eternal. Even the weather was depressing. For though it was 91 degrees one day and 50 the next, there was always a dust storm in the offing.

They all started the same way. I'd glance out the living room window or I'd traipse out to the clothesline, and suddenly I'd notice a band of red along the western horizon. At first I didn't know what it meant. I soon learned. It meant I had half an hour to bring in the clothes and seal all windows and doors.

I don't know why I bothered. Once the dust arrived, blocking out the sun and all but obliterating the houses across the street, there was nothing much to do except watch it sift through the cracks and gather on the windowsills. If I'd forgotten to make the bed, I'd see a line of red dust where the covers were turned back. If the cupboard doors were open, the dishes would be gritty and have to be washed before I could use them again.

David suffered the most. He choked and gasped and sneezed and snuffled. Finally I had to put him in his room with wet towels strung along the windowsill and the vaporizer shooting steam like an uncorked geyser.

"I don't know how much more of this I can take," I wrote Joe.

"If David isn't coughing and hacking because of the dust, the change in temperatures has given him another case of tonsillitis, and I'm rushing him down to Dr. Sullivan for a penicillin shot."

This wasn't the usual tone of my letters. I'd tried to make the bulk of my correspondence cheerful and uplifting, knowing as I did that *The Air Force Wife* disapproved of whining and complaining.

I'd omitted the long and gruesome story of my war with the repairman who, I suspected, was ordering parts from a tinsmith in Venezuela and having them delivered by raft.

I'd neglected to go into my run-in with Lieutenant Bussmeir when I tried to take David with me into the commissary. And I'd even neglected to mention my journey to the base vet's with Vicar.

It was a typical TDY event. One morning when I was picking up David's toys I suddenly noticed that Vicar was sitting in the corner shivering and foaming at the mouth. Because I vividly remembered a mad dog I'd seen as a child, and because it had foamed at the mouth too, I panicked immediately.

Naturally Ruth wasn't home that day. Neither was Phyllis Walker. Even weird Willard and Bunny were gone, on leave in Chicago, though I knew if he had been home he wouldn't have helped. Finally I called the base vet. On the eleventh ring someone answered.

"Mumble-mumble-mumble. Sir?"

"Is this the vet's office?" I asked, being in no mood to try translating his spiel.

"That's what I said, ma'am," he answered in a tone that told me he was in no mood for me either.

"Is the vet there?"

"No, ma'am."

"Well, maybe you can help." I explained my predicament in gruesome detail, taking care to be lavish with my superlatives in the futile hope he'd be moved to make a house call. I should have known better.

"Bring him in, ma'am," he said in a bored and nasal twang. "I can't tell what's wrong if I don't see him."

"But is it safe?" I asked. "I mean having him in the same car with my baby and all."

148

"I don't know, I guess so."

"Oh, well, thank you." I hung up.

By now Vicar seemed to have calmed down some, so I decided to risk it. First I bundled up David—this was one of the cold and windy days—and strapped him in his travel seat. Then I raced back in the house, put on Vicar's leash and led him out to the car. He wasn't thrilled with the prospect. When he saw what I had in mind he lay down on the grass, refusing to budge. So I pushed and tugged and did everything but carry him to the car. Finally I got him in. By now he was foaming at the mouth again, and I considered joining him.

Luckily it wasn't far to go, and I kept him fairly quiet in the back seat. But when I parked and opened the door, he leapt into the front, and only superb reflexes let me grab his leash before he escaped. David giggled and shouted, "Down, Dicker."

I looked around to see if I could spot anyone who'd help me get dog and child into the office together. The place was deserted. So I made an executive decision.

"I'll be right back," I told David. "I just have to get him into the office."

David gnawed on his fist and wiggled his toes, and I took off at a run.

The office was empty except for one airman who was reading a comic book.

"Is the doctor here?" I asked, keeping a close rein on Vicar, who was showing signs of hostility.

"Nah," he said. "He's on leave."

I should have known. He probably had word there was a locker full of rotting meat waiting for his inspection and decided to make a run for it.

"Well, can you do something?" I said, and ran through my whole story again.

He got up. "Sure," he said. "Just bring him in here and lift him on the table."

"I can't lift him," I said, wondering if he thought I was wearing maternity clothes simply because I was fat. "I'm pregnant."

"Oh." He thought a minute and stared at Vicar, who was not making the situation look easier. "Well, you can at least help. That hound looks vicious."

I resisted the impulse to complicate things further with a couple of acid remarks. "All right," I said, and together we went into the examining room and hefted him up onto the table. By now Vicar was in a real frenzy. The airman reached out to pat him, and he snapped.

"That's it," he said, stepping back from the table. "I'm not gettin' bit by no mad dog. You better take him downtown."

"But . . ." I protested.

"No, siree," he said again, tugging at the leash so Vicar had to jump to the floor. "I ain't takin' no chances. Sorry, lady. I wish I could help you, but you'll have to find someone else."

With that he handed me the leash and led us both to the door, making sure as he did to keep me between himself and Vicar. As he closed the door behind us, I mumbled a brief obscenity and went back to the car. This time Vicar was delighted to get in, and with a sigh of relief I saw David was still happy.

At the veterinary clinic downtown, I reversed the procedure, taking David in with me and leaving Vicar in the car. Once I'd explained the situation to the doctor there, I let him go out and bring the dog in. He seemed perfectly willing to do so, and David and I sat down in the waiting room.

After twenty minutes dog and doctor reappeared. Apparently they'd used a side entrance.

"Well, Mrs. Combs," the doctor said, "I gave him a shot, and I have some pills here you can give him once a day."

"What's wrong with him?"

"I don't know for sure. I think he's just nervous."

"Then it isn't rabies or anything like that?"

"Oh, no."

"And I don't have to worry about having him around the baby?"

"No, no. Just keep giving him these pills and he should calm down."

I thanked him verbally and with a sizable check, and his nurse helped me get my entourage back safely into the car.

"Well, troops," I said as we headed back out to the base, "it seems we've weathered another TDY crisis. And though I won't bother Daddy with the details now, just wait till he gets home. He's going to hear stories that will melt his brand-new captain's bars."

Of course by the time Joe did arrive, I was so delighted to see him all I could do was babble, "Gee it's good to have you home. Is there anything I can get you? How about a drink? Can I get your slippers? What would you like for dinner?"

That's one fringe benefit of TDY's. The homecomings are glorious.

15

I HAVE A FLOCK OF
STORKS ON RADAR, SIR

It was like an epidemic. Pregnancy was running rampant in the neighborhood. Everywhere you looked, June was busting out all over, and so was everyone else. I thought perhaps they'd added something to the base water supply. Joe said, no, it was a military tradition, like moving in June.

"Air Force wives always give birth in the summer," he maintained. "It's in the regulations."

"You're clever," I told him, "but I think I'll stick with the old cold winter, pregnant summer theory."

Still I had to admit he had circumstantial evidence on his side. For one thing, except for three of us, the other two being the Riebans and weird Willard, the neighborhood was a whole new crowd of people. For another, every other wife, it seemed, was wandering around in maternity clothes and with swollen ankles.

Along our stretch of pavement we'd substituted Bill and Mary Torell for the Frobishers, who'd finished out their American tour and had headed back to civilization with tea at four, bangers and mash for supper, and the BBC. Bob and Phyllis Walker had left in early May, this time for an assignment in Alaska. And in their place we had John and Betty Blymer. Then up the street, back door to back door with Willard and Bunny, were the Mattsons, Frank and Eleanor.

Out of these six families, three of us were due to give birth sometime before September. Eleanor was expecting in July. My ETA was mid-August, and Ruth was scheduled for September.

As luck would have it, the neighborhood was largely medical. Stan was the base pharmacist. Willard still labored under the theory he was a dentist, and both Frank and John were internists. Unfortunately Marge and Ted had not only moved out of the neighborhood, they'd also finished their tour and gone on to civilian practice in Salt Lake City. Had they been with us, Ted could have increased the coterie of physicians, and Marge could have joined the maternity ward.

As it was, we swelled our throng without her, and we relied on John and Frank to keep us current on hospital procedure; and because they, like Ted, were civilians at heart, they also kept us current on the latest in the world of red tape. They were more than equal to the task. When the heat drove us all out to the lawn in the evenings, to sit in the dark and fan ourselves, they entertained us with the latest goings-on.

"Today we had a mock disaster," Frank announced one night when we were sitting out by our back door.

"A mock disaster? What's that?" I took a sip of the lemonade Mary had made and brought over.

"It's like war games," Joe said, "only medical."

"I still don't understand."

"Let me explain," Frank continued. "What they do is this. They take an empty hangar, fill it with row upon row of supposed casualties."

"Where'd the casualties come from?" Mary asked.

"From a nuclear holocaust. You see, we're to pretend the base has been attacked."

"We're also to pretend it didn't wipe us off the face of the earth,"

John muttered, shaking his head disgustedly.

"Anyway," Frank said, "we've got all these bodies, and the purpose of the thing is for us to figure out which cases need medical attention, what kind of attention they need, and in what order we should treat them."

"Wait a minute." Mary held up her hand. "Where'd you get the bodies? I don't mean in the nuclear disaster; in the mock nuclear disaster."

"Oh, I don't know. It was one of the squadrons on base that volunteered to act as our victims." He paused to be sure we understood, then continued. "So they lined them up, each with a tag on his chest that tells what's wrong. And we had to sort through as fast as we could and save all their lives."

"Meanwhile," John said, picking up the narrative, "Colonel Brisker stood over in the far corner where they'd cleverly stashed all the cases marked critical. And he had his clipboard and his pen, and every couple of minutes he marked another body off as 'dead.' "

Frank laughed. "Hell," he said, "by the time I got over there they were all gone. The last one gave up the ghost just as I approached." He helped himself to some more lemonade. "Needless to say, we have another mock disaster next week."

"I think the whole thing's stupid." Eleanor bristled. "Haven't those jackasses got anything better to do with their time?" As a former nurse, she was less than tolerant when it came to what she considered military frivolity.

Normally Joe would have argued with her and made at least a halfhearted attempt at explaining the Air Force principle of readiness. Even Bill Torell, who wasn't given to idle comments, seemed about to say something. But both decided against it. They were wise. Approaching motherhood combined with the heat, and her general discomfort, had shortened her temper till like a dynamite fuse it sparked and sputtered and threatened to explode; and I doubt either could have escaped the fallout.

At least she wasn't terrified of actually giving birth, as Ruth was. Poor Ruth. She was the only offspring of a mother who claimed to have reached the pinnacle of life's pain during childbirth. While the rest of us had grown up hearing lullabies and stories of Cinderella,

Ruth had listened to tales about contractions and lower back misery. So, despite assurances from her doctors, she staggered through pregnancy with all the enthusiasm of a convicted felon.

Mary and I did our best to allay her fears. Mary had two little girls of her own, and David was living proof I'd been through the process before, so we joined forces and tried to convince her labor was the next best thing to a week in the Caribbean. We were meticulous in our efforts. We avoided the words "scream" and "agony." We never mentioned stitches unless we were referring to clothing, and we indulged in so many platitudes we sounded like verses two and three in a Mother's Day greeting card.

I doubt we helped, but at least we tried. And when all else failed we pointed to the charms of our own progeny and said, "How else can you be privy to such delight?"

We had to pick our moments. I didn't, for instance, call Ruth in to watch David refuse to go to sleep at night. And Mary, whose Sam was romping through her terrible twos, didn't publicize the tantrums, the sly pinches when Becky, the baby, was crying and Mary was looking elsewhere, and the attacks on Charlie, their long-suffering cocker spaniel.

Sam loved that dog. It was her pet, her toy, her confidant, and her nemesis. It allowed itself to be stuffed into a doll carriage and raced down the sidewalk. It fetched anything from crayons to pennies to Becky's pacifier. And once when it inadvertently swallowed one of the pennies it fetched, it put up with Sam's reaching her arm halfway down its throat and didn't retaliate.

Vicar never would have condoned such indignities. In fact, after his first attack of nerves, he became increasingly skittish, till finally we had to admit he was simply not cut out for life as a military dependent. Luckily someone up at Joe's office knew of a man out in the country who was willing to take him. So one Sunday in early June Joe snapped on his leash, herded him into the car, and delivered him to his new home. It was a tearful parting, but when Joe returned he assured me Vicar was delighted with his new lot in life.

"The minute I let him out of the car," he said, "he raced around the farm like a prisoner getting out of jail."

So though we missed him, we knew he was far happier, and life was certainly less complicated without his escapes, his attacks on the mailman, his predawn announcements that the paper had come, and his deposits on weird Willard's lawn.

As usual it was blisteringly hot that summer. The sun rose in the morning angry and seething. It blazed across the sky all day, searing plants and melting asphalt. And it set with a fury that dared night to bring relief. Eleanor bought two air conditioners, closed her blinds against the heat, and stayed inside. Ruth, like Phyllis before her, huddled in a cool back bedroom and only came out to hang up her laundry and complain of chronic indigestion.

Mary and I weren't so lucky. Small children don't take to spending the summer in a dark house with cold washcloths on their pressure points. They want to be out where the action is, running, jumping, digging, swinging, and crawling through the grass. So Mary hauled out Sam's wading pool, put it in the shade behind her house, and filled it up. Then she and I sat in lawn chairs, dangled our feet in the water, and supervised. It was active work, for though Sam leapt in and out safely and with ease, David, still an unsteady walker, tended to slide under the water if he got too excited, and Becky needed help just sitting up. Still it was worth it, for after an hour in the pool I stayed cool clear into evening.

"You know what," I said to Joe one afternoon when he'd slogged home from work with his hat plastered to his head and his uniform welded to his back, "we ought to get a wading pool of our own."

He took off his shirt and stood like a surrendering prisoner in front of the typhonic blast from our evaporative cooler. "You think so?" he said.

"Boy, do I." I handed him a cool drink. "For one thing, if we had one of our own, I could set it up anytime and not have to rely on Mary every day. And for another thing, you could sit in it too."

"I?"

"Sure."

"Aren't I rather large for a wading pool?"

"Well, I'm not saying you'd be able to do laps, but I'm sure you can find one a bit bigger than the Torells', and you could at least sit in it, and if I can get cool with just my feet submerged, surely you can with your seat under water."

"Don't be smart." He put his glass down on the table. "OK," he said after a while, "we'll do it. I'll get one on Saturday. I'll get the biggest wading pool I can find."

He did too. It measured ten feet across, was seventeen inches deep, and took two hours to fill. We set it up on the hill behind the house, right near the fence that surrounded the schoolyard. It was an instant success. Children came from blocks away. They brought pails and shovels, inner tubes, and rubber ducks. They came with their friends. They came with their neighbors. They dragged their baby sisters with them and shrugged when little Susie stepped out of her diapers and wandered around nude.

The only people they didn't bring were parents.

"Does your mother know where you are?" I'd ask someone barely two feet high who was demanding to be lifted in.

"Yep."

"Are you sure?"

"Yep. She told me, 'You go on down to the Combses' and swim. Mama's got a headache.' "

So Mary and Ruth, and sometimes Eleanor and I, sat around in a circle, like the witches in *Macbeth,* and tried to keep track of the children that were jumping in and out, falling down, showing off, trying to swim, and above all shrieking. David loved it. He held on to the edge and circumnavigated, bouncing up and down and chattering as he went.

After work, Frank and Stan and Joe joined the group. They usually displaced a goodly number of children, telling them their mothers were calling. They kept only enough for errands.

"Hey Jimmy, will you go down to my house in the kitchen and bring up two more beers?"

"Cindy, hand me those sunglasses over there, would you?"

"Has anyone seen my cigarettes?"

Bill Torell rarely ventured in. Mary said it was because as a native Southerner, from Georgia, he felt it was his patriotic duty to suffer silently with the summer heat. Weird Willard paid one official visit, but someone accidentally splashed water on his uniform and he left. John and Betty went on leave, so they were absent too.

When I wrote Mother and told her about our amusement park, she immediately sent David a Polaris underwater missile launcher, and suggested Joe could help show him how to use it. Joe claimed David was much to young to appreciate it, so he and Stan and Frank spent their weekends lounging in the pool, drinking beer, and launching missiles over the fence into the schoolyard. They let their gofers race along the fence, through the gate, and across the schoolyard to retrieve them.

By the time evening wandered along, everyone was cool, and since no one was anxious to go inside, where the heat still shimmered like a mirage, we pooled our resources, set up the barbecue, and slapped some hamburgers on the grill. Sometimes Ruth would bring a salad. Sometimes I would. Eleanor usually contributed potato chips and buns and carrot sticks, or else some lemonade. Then Mary and Bill cranked up their ice cream machine.

After we'd put the children to bed, we all brought out our home movies and colored slides, and bored each other with pictures of our weddings, movies of the Grand Canyon, and slides from San Francisco. Joe's and my from-the-waist-down wedding pictures were always a great hit, and every once in a while as a pièce de résistance we ran the reception movies backwards and showed Joe spitting up wedding cake.

Sometimes the sessions went on and on. Sometimes the enlisted men across the street complained about the noise, and the Air Police dropped by to suggest we call it a night. But no matter. By then it was usually time to scatter anyway.

As June melted into July, Eleanor's countdown began, and Ruth and I stepped up the frequencies of our visits to the doctor. We were all enrolled at the base hospital. David had been born downtown, but since then Congress had thrown one of its military spending fits, so now it was the base hospital or nothing.

On Saturday, July 25, Joe and I were awakened by a pounding on the front door.

"It's a girl," Frank shouted when Joe went to see who was there. "A seven-pound, ten-ounce baby girl."

"When?" I asked.

"At three this morning."

"How's Eleanor?"

"Fine, just fine."

We tried to get him to stay and have a cup of coffee, but he was too excited. Like Paul Revere, he still had every Middlesex village and farm to alert, so he galloped off and we went back to bed.

But once Eleanor had broken the maternal ice, I could hardly wait to get the whole thing over with too. The doctors shared my impatience.

"How'd you like some castor oil?" Dr. Marvin, the head of Obstetrics, asked one day in early August.

"No thanks."

"You sure?"

"Very sure. Besides," I added, "Joe would never approve. He and I are in the middle of a Scrabble tournament, and he's predicted I won't deliver till he's won 350 games."

"How many does he have to go?" he asked, playing along.

"Fifteen."

"Well, tell him he'd better get busy. This baby's not holding out much longer."

I did, and Joe being the real gentleman that he is, made me play till ten that night. Sorry to say, I won two of the five games, and by my next appointment he still had three victories to go.

This time I got Dr. Maxwell. He didn't care that Joe's championship had yet to be cinched.

"That child is ready to come, so here"—he handed me a prescription for castor oil—"Take this as soon as you get home and with luck I'll see you back by dinnertime."

"What are you all doing," I asked, "trying to get your deliveries over with so you'll have a free weekend?"

He laughed. "That's it," he said. "Now cooperate.,"

Joe had taken two weeks of leave, so he was home when I got there.

"Here we go," I said as I held my nose and swallowed. "This is supposed to do it."

Naturally it didn't, and by dinnertime I not only wasn't up at the hospital, I was exhausted from dealing with castor oil's normal side effects. This didn't impress Joe. He was determined to win his three games, so we sat up till he'd done so.

159

I think he took advantage of my weakened condition though, for his last victory hinged on an enormous score for the word, "zebulex."

"That's not a word," I said as he put the letters down.

"Of course it is," he insisted. "It's a fishing term."

"I don't believe you."

"Look it up then."

"But I don't know where the dictionary is."

"Well," he said, with an innocence politicians would kill for, "I guess you'll have to take my word for it then."

Normally I wouldn't have, but I was too tired to struggle.

"All right," I said, "but I'm going to check later, and if you're lying, you owe me three midnight feedings."

He agreed, probably because he knows my memory rivals my attention span for brevity. And we went off to bed.

When I woke up the next morning, I knew I'd not be home long. I got up. Joe was in the kitchen frying bacon. David was in his feeding chair demolishing a boiled egg and toast.

"I don't mean to make you nervous," I said, coming up behind Joe, "but I wouldn't count on having breakfast if I were you."

"Huh?"

"It's time to go."

"Are you sure?"

"I'm sure."

"All right," he said, sounding unusually calm. "Now let's see. You packed last night, so that's ready. I have to take David over to Mary's, and then we have to call Dr. Maxwell. Is there anything else?"

I stared at him. "Boy," I marveled, "you certainly are cool and collected. I thought you'd fall apart like last time."

"Why should I?" he snapped. "After all, I've been through this before. Now, I'll take David"—he lifted him out of his high chair— "and I'll be right back. Be ready."

I saluted. "Yes, sir."

Once in the car, his poise faltered slightly. Though we didn't have to pass through the gate and meet his old nemesis the guard, he fumed and fussed at the driver of the car in front of us who took his time making a left hand turn. Then he almost ran over a lady who was skittering across the intersection by the BX.

"Careful," I gasped.

"I am. I am."

Minutes later we turned into the hospital parking lot.

"Oh, damnit," Joe growled. "It's full."

"No, it isn't," I said, breathing through my mouth, trying to keep the pain to a minimum. "See, there are some spaces down there."

"Oh." He sped down to the other end of the lot.

"Oh, hell."

"What's the matter?"

"They're reserved."

"For whom?"

"For doctors."

"Can't we park there anyway? Isn't this considered an emergency?"

"No. They're reserved." He swung out of the lot. "But I'll go through again to see if anyone back there has pulled out."

They hadn't, and he swore again.

"Please, Joe," I said, "park in a doctor's space. You can leave a note on the window."

"No. I'll try that other lot across the way."

A car behind us honked.

"Shut up you idiot, I'm moving," Joe growled.

I turned around. It was Dr. Maxwell.

"Joe, he's waving us into his space," I pleaded.

But no. He chose to take another spin around the course. This time Dr. Maxwell was parked, out of his car, and flagging us down like a traffic cop.

"Pull in here," he yelled. "Don't worry, it's all right."

Joe did so, and we got out and rushed inside. Half an hour later Sylvia Ann—with a red face, a mop of black hair, and a magnificent set of lungs—was born.

"You were lucky," Dr. Maxwell said as the nurse showed her to me. "I thought for a while there that this delivery was going to take place in the parking lot."

"You think I was lucky," I told him. "You were the one who was lucky. "Joe might have made you salute too."

161

16

$\star$ $\bigstar$ $\star$ 16 $\star$ $\bigstar$ $\star$

OVER TO X-RAY AND
DOWN TO THE LAB

One thing about Air Force hospitals. It's best to be in the peak of condition if you're scheduled to check into one. For running the marathon is nothing compared to making the jaunt from Admissions, to Obstetrics, to X-ray, to the Lab, to the Pharmacy, and back again.

I think it's because the government was probably trying to save money when they built the first two or three hospitals. So rather than hire an architect, they told the man who'd laid out the airport runways to take a stab at designing the medical complex. He, of course, assumed they had admired the additional yardage he added for extended takeoffs, and the fact he'd allowed for cross winds. So he included these features in his hospital plans. Consequently most Air Force hospitals have all the convenience and intimacy of Kennedy International. The facilities at Sheppard were no exception.

The first thing you had to consider when contemplating an excursion to the military medicos for bronchitis or a broken leg or maternity care was how long you could stand the pain, for appointments

162

weren't handed out like aspirin prescriptions. Emergencies were handled in the emergency room, where a three-hour wait weeded out the hypochondriacs, and miracle cures occurred after about an hour and a half. Regular appointments called for the traditional phone call, with the regulation answer: "Mumble . . . mumble . . . mumble. Sir?" Then you were put on hold while the Gray Lady on duty took her morning coffee break. When she came back you were offered a choice between three weeks from Thursday at 0900 or the first of next month at 1100.

I always tried to take any nine o'clock appointment offered. It gave me a better shot at the token parking lot across the street from the front entrance. Of course there was always room in the main one, five blocks away, and once in a while a space or two along the street would open up. But as a rule if I got there early enough I could squeeze in between a nurse's station wagon and a corpsman's convertible.

Once inside the building, the procedure was standard. I checked in, accepted the news that an emergency had come up and no one knew when the doctor would be back, and settled down in the waiting room. I always came prepared with a book or two, for the assortment of reading material provided was not altogether inspiring. There were usually several copies of *Popular Mechanics,* the previous January's issue of *The Fisherman,* two or three hardcover editions of *Bible Stories for the Very Young,* and a couple of back issues of the *Reader's Digest.* These were so old, however, that the feature article was *I Am Joe's Diaper Rash.*

The main waiting room was where everyone—young, old, officer, enlisted man, and often the contagious—spent his first hour. There were elderly retired couples huddled together in the corner. There were maternity cases, awkward and uncomfortable on the metal folding chairs. There were field grade officers approaching retirement who were looking for an ailment to render their retirement income tax free. There were feverish babies and haggard mothers. And there was the inevitable two-year-old who lurched from one end of the room to another and paused only long enough to place a sticky hand on my knee.

"Hi," he'd burble.

163

"Hi," I'd make the mistake of answering. "What's your name?"

"Hi," he'd say again.

"Is that your mommy over there?" I'd ask, hoping it would spur him into joining her.

"Hi."

His mother usually ignored him, but occasionally she'd look up, yell, "Harold, you get back here or I'm going to slap you silly," and he'd stumble back to her dubious embrace.

Older children sat for a while swinging their legs back and forth and flipping through books faster than an Evelyn Wood graduate student. Every once in a while, if there was a brief silence, they'd speak up. "Mommy," they'd bellow, "what's wrong with that funny-looking man over there?"

After twenty minutes or so, someone would call my name, and I'd jump up. Maybe, just this once, I'd think, hoping against hope, I'd get through here before noon. This was silly. Of course I wouldn't get through before noon. I was only being summoned because the nurse had just discovered that my medical records were missing.

"They simply aren't here," she'd tell me in a tone that implied I was at fault. "So you're going to have to go to Records and get them."

Since it was either that or another extended conversation with the two-year-old, I jumped at the chance.

"Just go out the east door," she'd tell me, "then keep straight till the second intersection. Turn right there, left at Orthopedics, another right at the cast room, and it's the fifth door on your left."

I resisted the impulse to ask her if I might leave a trail of cracker crumbs, so I wouldn't get lost, and headed off.

By the time I got back, it was only forty minutes past the original time for my appointment. But hope sprang eternal as the nurse stapled everything together so I wouldn't cheat and look to see what diseases I'd had, then sent me off to Obstetrics.

This time I had to go out the west door, down the hall, past Surgery, the staff dining room, and Wards A, B, and C, till I came to another waiting room. This one was peopled solely by women in various stages of pregnancy, and when I went in I handed my records to the nurse at the main desk.

"Ah, yes, Mrs. Combs," she'd say. "Step right over here for your weight and blood pressure."

This was the signal for everyone in the room to stop in mid-conversation and listen to see how much the latest victim weighed. It would have been hard to miss hearing it, for military nurses work in pairs. One fiddles with the scales, making a production of the fact she has to add an extra weight to the balance. The other sits across the room with pencil poised. When the machine stops vibrating and settles down, the first nurse hollers, "Combs, Ann G. One hundred and . . ." and everyone nods, delighted because you've gained more than they have.

I always prepared for the weigh-in with the precision of someone contemplating an ascent up Mount Everest. We all did. Every piece of clothing we wore was the lightest of its species. In the middle of January neighbors could tell we were headed to a doctor's appointment because we left the house clad in sandals and a summer cotton. We also threw off our coats and leapt out of our shoes the minute our names were called. And as a casual observer strolling by the Obstetrics waiting room often did a double take and asked, "Is it summer already?"

After the weigh-in it was back to waiting, and back to reading my book, since the literature on hand didn't improve. In fact it usually consisted of cast-offs from the main waiting room plus a series of pamphlets on hemorrhoids and varicose veins.

I didn't bring just any book with me. I was careful in my selection, especially after the month I inadvertently caused a mild sensation by settling down and opening up *By Love Possessed*. Even the head nurse, traditionally the epitome of a granite Florence Nightingale, allowed the flicker of a smile to pass over her face that day. And the woman sitting next to me poked me in the ribs, pointed to the title, and said, "You're not just a-kidding, sweetheart."

The next step in the interminable trek toward "Fine, Mrs. Combs. Everything's fine. See you next week" was a call to a chair in the hall outside the doctor's office.

This was always exciting because it was the first clue as to what doctor I'd be seeing. It might be Dr. Rothgill, who prided himself on the fact he kept a hand warmer in his pocket so he wouldn't punch and probe with icy fingers up and down your spine.

It might be Dr. Bitterman, who hated the Air Force, Texas, heat, women, and orderlies, in rotating order.

It might be Dr. Marvin, head of Obstetrics and a career officer, who like others who'd chosen the military life over private practice had a certain, casual "You know I don't really need your business" attitude.

Or it might be Dr. Maxwell. He, like Frank, Ted, and John, was merely serving his time. So he kept his skills and his bedside manner honed for later life on the outside. It was a lucky day when I got him.

Usually, however, I drew Dr. Bitterman, and I knew I was in for at least one tirade. It might be a blanket condemnation of pregnant women, who, he claimed, do nothing but eat and bitch. He might be chafing under the strain of having been on duty all night. Or he might be upset because his coffee was cold. Whatever the reason, he was always snarling about something.

I think he'd chosen his nurse himself, for she was no more enthusiastic about life than he, and when she called out my name I sprang to.

"All right," she'd bark, leading me into the examining room, "take off your clothes; put them on that chair over there. Put this gown on, and the doctor will be with you as soon as he can."

Then she'd stride out of the room in search of another victim.

I don't know what it is about Air Force nurses. I've seen them away from the hospital decked out in soft hairdos, form-fitting dresses, and stiletto heels. I've seen them talk, laugh, even flirt. And I've seen them speak kindly to small children and stop to pat a dog on the head. But somehow once they go on duty, they yank their hair back into a Puritan knot, clamp on a starched uniform, stuff their feet into the Air Force version of British walking shoes, and don an expression that would make Grendel's mother look pleasant.

Dr. Bitterman's nurse was the queen of the harridans, and when she snapped, "Take off your clothes and put them on the chair," I did as I was told. It wasn't exactly easy. The chair, always a gray metal folding chair, was in the corner of the room. The standard operating procedure at this point was to stand next to it, pull a curtain that hung on rings from a track in the ceiling around you, and then undress. It would have been simpler to leave the curtain open, since it had been hung to surround the chair and nothing else. Simpler, yes; wiser, no. For as I'd learned from sad experience, examining rooms were often visited by nurses, orderlies, janitors, or anyone else who might be wandering down the hall.

Once my hospital gown was on, and I'd hidden my dingy slip under my skirt on the chair, I ventured out and hiked myself up onto the examining table to wait.

Naturally the wait was long. So I busied myself trying to read the small print on the full color diagram of the pelvis that was on the wall across the room. When that palled I switched to counting tongue depressors, throat swabs, and sometimes the dots on the acoustical ceiling. I would have leapt down and gotten my book, but that meant another leap when the doctor and the nurse returned, and in a gown with southern exposure it was not a pretty sight. Besides, Dr. Bitterman's nurse did not approve of reading, and I wasn't about to annoy her more than absolutely necessary.

As a rule the examination, once it finally took place, was brief, and before I knew it I was back behind the curtain struggling into my clothes. This time the nurse stuck around. Supposedly she was getting ready for the next patient. Actually she stayed to make sure I didn't dawdle. It worked. With her clearing her throat and clanging instruments on the other side of the curtain, I dressed faster than a stripper in a police raid. Consequently I usually left with my stockings on backwards and my collar half in and half out.

After the hilarity of my encounter with Dr. Bitterman and his dyspeptic nurse, nothing would have pleased me more than to have been left to find my way back to daylight, fresh air, and my car. This, however, was rarely my fate. There was usually a two-mile hike to the Lab for blood work, occasionally a back track with a dogleg to the right for X-rays, and then a final sprint to the pharmacy for a prescription. By then it was almost time for my next appointment.

The delivery room, when I finally graduated to that step of my maternal adventure, was even more fun. Not only were there doctors and nurses wandering in and out, and other women groaning behind the room divider, there were also little clutches of orderlies standing around the room looking bored. Some were so young their acne hadn't cleared, and if I hadn't been essential to the whole process I would have preferred waiting out in the hall till it was over.

In 1959, when Sylvia was born, saddle blocks were the anesthetic of the day. Since then they've offered women a choice. But at the time it was saddle block or a swig of bourbon and a bullet. I chose a saddle block. This, of course, meant eight hours in the recovery room, lying still with my head down.

"If you don't," one of the nurses warned, "you're going to end up with headaches you wouldn't believe."

I knew she meant business. Eleanor had already described the consequences of sitting up and moving around. So I lay still. But it was a long rest. The hours dragged by like months. They let Joe in for a brief "Hi, honey. The baby's beautiful," but then they made him leave. I wasn't tired, so I didn't sleep and wake up to find that time had galloped by. Lunch, though a challenge, since it had to be eaten out of the side of my mouth, didn't take up more than twenty minutes. And as the afternoon wore on I found myself longing for just one ancient copy of *Popular Mechanics* or the *Reader's Digest*.

Finally, however, in the late afternoon the nurse came to tell me my ordeal was over and I could go to the ward.

"You mean I'm through here?" I asked, sitting up gingerly.

"Yep. Here's your slippers and your bathrobe, and there's the door."

"Great," I said, waiting for her to help me down the hall or put me in a wheelchair or something.

I should have known better.

"Now up you get," she prodded. "Can't stay here all day."

I struggled to my feet and we walked out into the hall.

"See there?" she said. "That door down there?"

I nodded.

"That's the maternity ward. Just go on down, and the ward nurse'll give you a bed. Better hurry though," she added. "Dinner's in half an hour."

So with her blessing I set off on another journey of a thousand steps.

"Good Lord, girl!" the ward nurse exclaimed when I stumbled in the door. "Where'd you come from?"

I ran my hand through my disheveled hair. "Recovery," I said.

"Whooee." She whistled through her teeth. "You're a sight. Why don't you take these clean pajamas and go back down the hall a ways and have yourself a shower?"

"Why not?" I muttered, turning around and heading back whence I'd come. "And after that shall I run down to the Lab and over to the Pharmacy?"

"Pardon?"

"Oh, nothing. I'll see you."

I had to admit it did feel good to get clean and cool, and after a dinner that while not inspiring was at least nutritious I was ready for another trek down, around the bend, and to the nursery.

I was less eager at 0200 when the nurse flung open the ward door, snapped on the overhead light, and bellowed, "OK, ladies, get your babies."

Joe came to visit whenever they let him. But Joe does not visit well. After a "How are you?" "How are things going?" and "What did they give you for lunch?" (or dinner, depending on the time of day) he recited what had been going on at home and then started checking his watch to see if perhaps it wasn't time to go.

At first he was blatant about it. He swung his arm around and stared at his watch. But when I, who'd spent the afternoon with nothing to do but listen to Mrs. Albion describe her Caesarian, complained, he resorted to more surreptitious methods.

One was the "Oh, my, I'm stiff" maneuver. This called for clasping his hands together, stretching them up over his head, then throwing his head back to sneak a look at his watch. Another was the "Good grief, my shoes are untied" strategy.

But the one that signaled his imminent departure was the "David and I sure do miss you" ploy. To accomplish this he'd look at me soulfully and reach his wristwatch arm out to pat my hand. When he did this, it was only a matter of minutes before he'd stand up and say, "Well, if I'm going to have time to take a peek in the nursery at Sylvia and get home to put David in bed, I'd better be off."

After that there was no holding him.

Luckily though, Joe's visits weren't my only link with the outside world. Sheppard, unlike most military hospitals, allowed other visitors. So when Joe disappeared I wasn't left to stare at other husbands hovering solicitously over their wives' beds. Mary came up twice. She warned me to play down any pain or discomfort should Ruth appear, since Ruth, with her time approaching, was getting more than edgy. Then she filled me in on the news of the neighborhood. Willard had tried to make a citizen's arrest when someone sped by his house, but they ignored him. Eleanor was exhausted from being up all night with Cindy, and she might not make it up to see me. Joe and Frank had shot a missile out of our pool that landed on Stan's roof, but they finally got it down. And Bill had received his orders.

"That means we'll be leaving in December for South Carolina," she said.

"Damn," I said, "why couldn't Willard and Bunny be leaving instead?"

"Actually I'm delighted," she told me. "Of course we'll miss you all, but it will certainly be a relief to get out of Texas."

I had to admit she had a point there.

Ruth's visit was brief, and I handled it expertly. I edged her away from Mrs. Albion as soon as possible and took her with me on a hike to the nursery. She was impressed.

"Boy," she said as we wandered back to the ward, "you don't seem to be any the worse for wear. Maybe having babies isn't as bad as I thought."

"Bad?" I said, giving a little skip to show I was agile and pain free. "It's a cinch."

"That's wonderful," she marveled. "That's really wonderful." Then she picked up her purse and left, humming as she went.

The minute she was out of sight my stitches and I crawled back in bed and lay very still till the throbbing subsided.

"Let her find out for herself what a cinch it is," I muttered to Mrs. Albion.

"And how."

And she did, six weeks later, when she gave birth to a son. She wasn't pleased with the revelation, and though I pleaded innocence, insisting I thought giving birth was the next best thing to a masquerade ball, and staying in a military hospital was like a vacation, I doubt she believed me. Why should she? I was lying.

$$\star \quad \bigstar \quad \stackrel{\wedge}{\curvearrowright} \quad 17 \quad \stackrel{\wedge}{\curvearrowright} \quad \bigstar \quad \stackrel{\wedge}{\curvearrowright}$$

30 DAYS,
4,000 MILES

Vacations are not taken lightly in the military, at least they didn't used to be. During my hitch there was none of this "Well folks, see you in a couple of weeks. Don't work too hard without me" so prevalent in the civilian world. Military men didn't saunter out of the office on Friday afternoon and check back in on a Monday morning several weeks later.

They were precise. Leaves began at 0001. They ended two weeks or a month later at 2359 and every second in between was spent en route to or from somewhere.

Joe and I had taken several leaves together in the two and a half years we'd been married. Both times we'd driven home to Bainbridge Island, a destination that was a mere 2,042 miles away. The first time we had Vicar as a passenger, and I learned how to smuggle a dog into a motel and how to look nonchalant when at a service station in the middle of Salt Lake City said dog lifted his leg at the pump.

The second trip was when David was two months old. On this jaunt I learned that small babies find riding in a car conducive to rest and enormous amounts of sleep. That is why they're so bright and energetic after sixteen hours on the road when you finally pull into a motel. Of course they know all you want to do is take a shower and fall into bed. But it doesn't matter. For them it's time for food, play, talk, and a little screaming if necessary.

I also learned that husbands and fathers tend to think that because they did the driving, and they forget you pleaded to be allowed to take the wheel, that they're exempt from child care. Consequently when you crawl into a hot tub they hand you the baby, saying, "Here you might as well bathe him too." While you warm a bottle and stir up some oatmeal and puréed peas, they lie down for a nap. While you march up and down the motel room cooing and pleading with your child to go to sleep, they snore. And when you burst into tears, sob that you hate every bone in their reclining body, and swear you wish you'd never married, they turn over and ignore you.

Joe and I prepared for all our leaves in the same way. We decided on a date, alerted relatives, who in retrospect probably would have preferred any other news, and started packing.

On the appointed day, while Joe went to work as usual, I finished the preparations. Naturally I worked from a list. There were clothes to be worn when we got there under one heading, and clothes to be worn on the trip under another. The children's things were divided into categories. Food was one. This included tiny boxes of cereal, jars of mashed bananas and veal purée, and four day's supply of formula. Another was clothing, with shirts, jackets, diapers, blankets, shoes, socks, dresses, bibs, pajamas, footed stretch suits, towels, and washcloths. I included only enough to get us from one laundromat to another. Then there were toys and stuffed animals and teething biscuits and storybooks. The miscellaneous category included maps, sunglasses, a thermos of hot coffee, wet towels, a diaper bag, aspirin, and a first aid kit.

All day long I assembled things and put them near the front door. All day long I made David put his teddy bear back and folded up the latest batch of diapers fresh in off the line.

When Joe got home we had dinner, did the dishes, and put the children to bed as if it were any other night. Then Joe went out and converted the back of the station wagon into a combination bed and playpen. He folded down the back seat, lined suitcases around the side, and filled the middle with blankets, pillows, and pads from the playpen. It didn't take him long. He was usually through by eight-thirty. So then we sat and stared at each other till midnight.

Five minutes before the clock struck twelve, Joe swooped off to the squadron orderly room to check out, and then roared back to get us. Then we transferred the children from their bed to the car and drove off into the night toward Highway 287 and points west.

The first leg of the journey was from Wichita Falls to Amarillo. It was 123 miles, and I can't remember ever having traveled it in the daylight. To me it will always be a ribbon of black studded with headlights from trucks and vans roaring east. And Amarillo itself will always be a diner just to the west of town that serves bacon, eggs, a side order of hash browns, and hot black coffee at five-thirty in the morning.

As a rule we took our leaves in the summer. It was swelteringly hot and dusty, but all the mountain passes between Texas and Seattle were open; and once we got to Bainbridge, with cool breezes off the water and nights brisk enough for blankets, it seemed worth it.

No one in his right mind would attempt the journey in December. I thought that then. I think it still. But when Sylvia was four months old and Christmas was coming, and it had been over a year since we'd been north, we decided it was a splendid plan.

We were wrong. We only had two weeks in which to make the round trip. We knew that icy roads and snow-blocked passes lay ahead. The children, both still babies, weren't used to long trips. And in all truth we really couldn't afford it. But who considers truth when life is monotonous and adventure beckons?

The first inkling that the gods of travel were not on our side came as we drove through Iowa Park, a little town about ten miles west of Wichita Falls. Sylvia woke up screaming. I think she realized we were traveling, and had decided to get into the swing of things by getting a case of traveler's digestion with all its ramifications.

At home it would have been inconvenient. On the road it was

also calisthenic. For in order to tend to her needs I had to rearrange everything in the front seat, and move the thermos from its position between my ankles to a safe place propped on the seat. Then I had to flip around, kneel on the front seat, and reach back to the diaper and clean clothes supply.

It would soon become the posture of the day, and by the time Joe's leave was over, I would realize I'd backed my way out of eight states of the union, and had spent seven days watching where I'd been. Sometimes, however, my knees rebelled, so I either turned back around, dragging Sylvia with me, or else I sat side-saddle and stretched my arm back to pat, soothe, and cajole. Too much of this cut off the circulation in my arm. But it was easier than holding her, for unlike David, who was often content to sit in my lap for hours at a time, she struggled to be off and exploring. There were knobs on the dashboard to be fiddled with and tugged at. There was the flashlight to be waved about, skimming it past my head. There were buttons on my clothes to be ripped off and flung to the floor. And there was always Daddy to reach for.

I pointed this adoration out to Joe. I told him his daughter was longing to have him hold her and tell her his apocryphal tales about the Korean war and how he'd bombed a cow. But he declined to switch places. He claimed he wanted to, but insisted he could hear a strange pinging in the engine, and didn't think I should be driving if it blew up.

So I continued to hold Sylvia, and on the few occasions when she agreed to lie in the back and play with her feet, David took advantage of my inactivity and slid over the back into the front seat, then climbed up me like a fireman scaling a ladder, and vaulted into the back again.

It was a wonderful game and gave me bruises that made me look as if I'd been run over by a tribe of marauding Pygmies. But every now and then, when the moon was waning and the wind was just right, they both slept, and I was free to return to my duties as navigator.

These duties weren't limited to checking the map to be sure we hadn't made a wrong turn somewhere sending us hell bent for Mexico. It was up to me to compute mileage, an occupation for which I

175

was sadly lacking. I had to monitor the radio, finding new stations as the old ones crackled into the distance. I was in charge of pouring coffee, and holding the cup between swallows. And most important, I was the motel and restaurant lookout.

This wasn't a simple "Oh, there's a place that looks good" activity. Joe, like most military men, believed in the supremacy of mileage. Eight hundred a day was his customary goal, and my insistence we stop every six hours or so interfered with his achieving this goal. So he set up rules.

The first was "Only restaurants on the right hand side of the road will be considered." He'd had a friend who crossed the street once, to eat at a famous Mexican restaurant in Santa Fe, and when the man and his wife came out, they were so relaxed and pleasantly full, they jumped in their car and headed back the way they'd come. They lost an hour and a half driving time, only making six hundred miles that day, and the horror of it all haunted Joe.

His second rule stated, "No restaurant is worth backtracking for." This meant I had to spot a place in the distance, decide, as we approached at sixty miles an hour, if it was a greasy spoon, a place that might not take well to rumpled travelers, or a place that looked inviting. Then I had to shout, "There's one. Right over there. Stop."

Most of the time Joe outfoxed me.

"I see one," I'd yell.

"Where?"

"Right up ahead. It's the one with the blue roof and the parking lot next to it."

"I still don't see it."

"It's . . . back there."

"Sorry, honey, but we've already passed it now. You have to let me know sooner. Don't worry though, the sign says its only forty miles to the next town."

He was even more particular about motels. As we entered a town, there were usually two or three on every block. Each one offered more amenities than the last. Wake-up calls, phones in the room, coffee and the paper delivered to your door in the morning. None would do.

"I want to get to the other side of town," he'd say. "That way

176

we won't get stuck in traffic when we leave."

"Traffic?" I'd shout. "But Joe, we get up at three or four in the morning. How much traffic do you expect at that hour?"

"You never know. Trucks drive all night, and we might get stuck behind a convoy of semis heading west."

Naturally the other side of town never had anything but manufacturing plants and warehouses. So because the no-backtracking rule applied to motels too, we'd go on to the next town, where we were lucky if we could find a place with an inside toilet.

At times, however, in my eagerness to reach food and water, I misjudged their eagerness to have us. Such was the case when Joe and I and our two boisterous passengers pulled into Albuquerque on that first day of our Christmas trip home.

It was noon on a Sunday, and as we drove through town, stomachs growling and heads swiveling like lighthouse beacons, we could see that the city like a family Bible was piously closed and locked.

"There's got to be some place that's open," I said. "Surely the good people of Albuquerque dine out occasionally on Sunday."

"I don't know," Joe said. "It doesn't look like it."

"Could we go back—on another street?" I asked, knowing full well that what I was suggesting was clearly against rules. "Just this one time?"

"Well," he said, trying not to let on he too was starving, "perhaps just this one time."

So we did. We retraced our steps. We drove on parallel streets, and we crisscrossed. Finally, just as we were about to give up, I spied an old hotel with a tiny blinking sign in the window.

"There's a place," I yelled.

"Where?"

"Up there. See?" I pointed, and Joe, who saw it too, pulled over and swooped into a waiting parking place.

"I thought we'd never find one," he said as he turned off the motor.

"Me either," I said, "but let's not waste time talking. I'm so hungry I could eat the upholstery."

It took a while to get our shirts tucked in and to change the children's diapers, find their coats in the tangle of blankets and pillows, and wipe off their faces. And I of course had to comb my hair, put on some lipstick, and try to pick off some of the lint I'd attracted in the five hundred miles since Wichita Falls. But finally we were ready, so we each grabbed a child, locked the car, and headed off down the block.

The moment we walked in the hotel I suspected we'd made a mistake. There was a certain formal air about the place, a brittle stodginess that whispered, "Leave quietly and don't make a scene." Unfortunately we were too hungry to listen, and when we located a small sign that said "Dining Room" we walked in.

The room was full. Obviously the faithful had risen at dawn, bathed and brushed and combed and polished. Then they had stepped into their Sunday best and hurried off to church, where they prayed for the poor, the unfortunate, the misguided, and the seedy. We fell into the last category, dressed as we were in rumpled traveling clothes, and as we came in an unspoken "Humph" rippled through the diners, and I found myself being glared at over bifocals and trifocals and granny glasses.

"Now I know how the publican felt in the Pharisee's church," I muttered to Joe. "Let's get out of here."

But Joe is not one to be easily cowed. He shifted Sylvia, who was happily cooing in her infant seat, to his other hip. "Why should we?" he said. "We're fine. Besides," he added as an aged maitre d' creaked over, "nothing else is open."

"May I help you?" the man said in a tone that suggested he hoped we were lost and only asking directions to the Salvation Army soup kitchen.

"Yes," Joe said, "we'd like a table."

"Oh"—he sniffed—"very well." He led us to a small table in the corner, handed us two menus, and retreated hastily.

We tried to settle in inconspicuously, and when the waitress came we ordered in hushed tones. It didn't help. That lunch lasted longer than most lifetimes. Each glass of water, each sandwich, napkin, coffee cup, and relish tray was placed on the table like a bowl of scraps being left for a stray dog. Every bite had its audience and I found myself chewing as if I had dynamite caps in my fillings.

David and Sylvia behaved themselves admirably. He didn't leap down out of his chair and race around the dining room. She refrained from throwing her bottle at the elderly couple at the next table. And neither of them raised their voices above a sepulchral hush. It wasn't enough. Two by two the diners finished their meals, dabbed at the corners of their mouths with linen napkins, edged their chairs back, and, giving us a wide berth, wended their way out.

Finally we did the same, and as we walked to the door there was a collective sigh of relief. I swear I also heard the maitre d' announce, "Ladies and gentlemen, the crisis has passed," but Joe says I made that up.

As we headed out of town, Joe added another rule of the road: No stopping at old hotel dining rooms.

We stayed the night in Gallup, on the far side of town, in a motel cleverly situated two giant steps from the railroad track. All night long trains roared through, and by dawn I'd almost mastered the art of sleeping while sitting bolt upright with my eyes peeled open.

The next morning we headed north, through our first set of mountains. Just as we feared, it started to snow as we approached Cortez in the southwest corner of Colorado.

"Here it comes," Joe groaned as he slowed to a crawl and peered through the flakes that were outwitting the windshield wiper. "We're in for it now."

"You mean you think we'll have snow from now on?" I asked.

"Yep. It'll probably be worse in the mountains east of Salt Lake, and chances are we'll get stuck in eastern Oregon or the Cascades."

"Are you sure?"

"I'm sure."

Joe comes from a long line of folk directly descended from Chicken Little, and each misfortune is looked on as only a taste of what's to come. So when we inched our way into town, he pulled into the first gas station, and pleaded with the attendant to put on our chains.

"That way we may be able to make it through the snowdrifts ahead," he told him.

The man was unimpressed, but what did he care if this wild-eyed man thought there were ten-foot drifts up the road? "No problem," he said. "Just drive right onto the rack, and we'll lift the car up and have them on in a jiffy."

Joe did so, and as soon as we were on the rack he got out. It's

179

SOP (standard operating procedure) in gas stations. Leave the premises immediately and leave the second in command to handle the troops. Before I could whistle him back and plead imminent uremic poisoning if I wasn't allowed a chance at the ladies' room, the car was rising.

This delighted David. "Look," he squealed. "Look at Daddy. Hi, Daddy."

I opened the window partway and held on to him tightly as he waved and chattered and pelted Joe with toys. Sylvia joined in the merriment and jabbered incoherent sentences in the back. And the mechanic dodged flying teddy bears and Lincoln logs, and snapped the chains into place.

Naturally the snow disappeared when we were two miles out of town, and we never saw any more. But Joe justified his actions, telling me it was impossible to be too careful.

Late that afternoon we drove into Salt Lake City. We'd warned Marge and Ted we were coming, and after a short phone call for directions, we pulled into their driveway.

It was a typical Air Force reunion.

"How's weird Willard?"

"Have you seen Tom or Dr. Kohary lately?"

"Any improvement in the commissary's vegetable selection?"

"Remember the time we . . ."

We sat up for hours drinking wine, reliving dust storms, and filling each other in on what had happened since. But in the morning we were on our way again. Because even Joe didn't have the nerve to rouse everyone for his traditional 3:00 A.M. getaway, we headed out around nine, and immediately took a wrong turn that almost shot us back to Albuquerque. Luckily we discovered our mistake, and soon we were back on the road speeding across the desert on our way to Boise.

By now we'd settled into a routine, and I'd perfected my various roles of the road as mother, navigator, co-pilot, tour director, wife, and librarian. It hadn't been easy. One minute I was on my knees changing a diaper or searching through the debris for a missing teething biscuit. The next I had to flip back and check the mileage between Payette and Huntington. One minute I was reading, "Once

180

there was a furry little cat with green eyes," and the next I was reciting the pertinent statistics for the Highway Rest Motel. I constantly scanned the horizon for cows, horses, barns, trains, and planes so I could divert David, who'd become so adept at vaulting into the front and scaling me on his return trip, that he could do it in five seconds flat.

At the end of the day, however, nothing amused, nothing pleased, nothing diverted. The last half hour, no matter when we stopped, was a medley from both children of complaints—howling, clamorous, inconsolable complaints. Trying to get to the motel before they reached a crescendo was like trying to outrun a flash flood. It was impossible.

So finally, when after four days on the road we crossed the bridge that connects Bainbridge to the mainland and sped down the length of the island to home and Mother, all I could think of was: At last . . . relatives to take over.

I wasn't disappointed. In the short time we were there, Mother took David with her when she went anywhere. Aunts and uncles attempted to hold Sylvia, and played peek-a-boo and patty cake with her. Daddy, an Englishman of the old school who believes that children should be brought into the parlor for a brief visit before they leave for boarding school, unbent slightly and did a few barnyard imitations at Christmas Eve dinner.

And then, what seemed like seconds after we'd arrived, we were on our way again. This time we headed south through Oregon and California with a sharp left at Bakersfield, a stop scheduled in Phoenix and El Paso, then a dogleg left across Texas to Wichita Falls.

This time I was prepared. The family doctor at home gave me a mild tranquilizer to dose out to the children when I could stand the noise no longer. I had new books to read them, new toys to delight them with, and a new map to monitor for Joe.

"This part of the trip is going to be a breeze," I told Joe as we waved goodbye and headed up the island.

I should have known better. It was merely variations on the original theme. True we didn't run into any snow, so I didn't get dizzy staring down from a mechanic's rack while he put on chains. But when we wove our way through the Siskiyous and David insisted

I read Edward Lear's "A was once an apple-pie, Pidy, Widy, Tidy, Pidy, Nice Insidy, Apple-pie," waves of nausea washed over me.

True, I had a tranquilizer to simmer down the children during that last half hour when we could stand it no longer. But the doctor had forgotten to warn me one dose might pep them up, so to go ahead and administer another. So when I fed them the magic elixir, and sat back with all the faith of a born-again Christian waiting for them to slow down, they didn't. They carried on, fussing, screaming, howling, yelling, and whining for two hours more.

True, Joe agreed to stop at a motel in the center of Phoenix. But the sumptuous one he chose took one look at him, one look at us huddled in our dusty car at their front door, and they fabricated a convention of plumbers, and sent us to a place more fitting to our obvious station in life.

True, we made excellent mileage on the last stretch from El Paso to Wichita Falls. But it would have been better if we hadn't had to change a flat tire, and run our car into a garage for a wheel alignment in Snyder.

By the final dash for the finish line, it was night, and once we passed through Iowa Park with twenty minutes to go, I knew we had a chance. Another flat on the Sheppard Access Road would have been our undoing, but fortunately our luck held out. At two minutes before 2400 Joe raced up the steps of the orderly room to check in.

We waited in the car. Then we drove home. Both children had been asleep for several hours, and for once Sylvia stayed that way as Joe carried her in and put her in bed.

David, however, woke up just as I carried him through the front door. For a minute he looked as if he couldn't believe his eyes. It was home . . . the place he'd assumed we'd left forever. With a squeal of delight he wriggled out of my arms and staggered across the room to where his enormous white stuffed bear was sitting vigilantly in the playpen. Then he tugged it out of the playpen and fell on it joyfully.

"Bear," he cried. "Bear."

Then he leapt up and, dragging it with him, padded off around the house checking each room, each door, each piece of furniture to be sure it was true. To be sure at last he was home.

Eventually we persuaded him it was time to go to bed. Bear went with him of course, and took up most of the bed. And after they'd snuggled down together, and I'd covered them up, Joe turned off the light.

"Well, well," he said as we wandered off to our own room, "we made it through another leave." He thought a minute, figuring. "Do you realize what mileage we made coming back?" he said. "Let's see . . . it was how far to San Francisco?"

"Sorry," I said as I stumbled out of my clothes and crawled into bed, "my hitch as a navigator is up. I'm retired. If you want to know the mileage, figure it out yourself."

☆ ★ ☆ 18 ☆ ★ ☆

THREE MOVES
EQUAL A FIRE

Legend has it that Murphy, the renowned author of the postulate "Anything that can go wrong will," was an Air Force captain. I believe it. I also suspect it was probably he who, after being transferred from base to base, once stood in the living room of his new quarters, surveyed his household goods, and first uttered the words "Three moves equal a fire."

If he didn't he should have, because it's true. Tornadoes may rage above your house, skipping through the base like a child on his way home from school. Dust storms may sift through the cracks under the door and settle forever in the fabric of your furniture. And floods may lap at your back door. But nothing in nature equals the destructive power of a move from one house to another, one base to another, or one country to another.

The government speaks in honied tones about PCS (permanent change of station) moves.

"You haven't a worry in the world," they gush. "We have contracts with movers all over the nation. A meticulous and highly trained crew will tiptoe into your home, quickly and quietly bundle up all your belongings, and be waiting for you at the other end of the line."

The movers themselves are less mellifluous. They hate their line of work. And right away you realize that the only way you could possibly please them would be by saying, "I've changed my mind. I'm staying right here. Why don't you boys take the day off and go fishing?"

It's immediately apparent, even on the preliminary visit when they're only casing the joint to determine how many cartons they need.

"Chees," they say as they stomp through the house leaving oily footprints on the rug, "you sure have a lot of crap here. If I were you I'd throw half this stuff out."

If you fail to be intimidated by that, and don't rush to decrease your inventory by chucking the bentwood rocker and the roll-top desk, they regale you with tales of horror from the movers' manual.

"Do you know what happens when a moving van has a flat tire in the desert?" they ask.

"No, what?"

"The temperature climbs to a hundred and twenty inside the van, and all the glue on your furniture dries up and the stuff falls apart."

"Perhaps so," you say, mentally tracing the route your goods will follow, "but our shipment won't be going through the desert."

"Oh, I wouldn't count on that," they reply. "If your junk doesn't fill up a whole van we may have to pick up another load, and God knows where they'll send us for that."

If that doesn't make you offer to leave everything where it is and start anew at your next base, they take turns telling you about the time when . . .

The time when the brakes failed on the hill going into Denver, and the driver barely managed to leap clear before the van careened into a brick wall.

The time when the goods were sent to the wrong base, and it took seven months to locate them again.

The time when a Teamsters' strike kept shipments idle for weeks.

185

I personally have heard stories that would make even a gypsy pack in his tambourine and settle down.

One horrendous tale concerned a foreman whose buddy had been killed by a falling Steinway. The man claimed he was reminded of the tragedy because I'd just asked him to put our old practice piano in the rec room in the basement. And when I rejected his suggestion that it stay upstairs and be the focal point of the living room, he told me he felt I should know what might happen if I insisted on having my way.

I was unimpressed. By then I'd moved several times, and I was immune to van lines scare tactics. I did pale however when he heaved a sigh and ordered the smallest man in his crew to attach a strap to the back of the piano, then wrap it around his neck and tie the other end to the front. And I rushed to cower in another room when I heard the shout "OK, Charlie, we're going to edge it down. You stay up at the top, and if it slips you can break the fall."

Fortunately it didn't slip, and heads didn't roll, but from that day on I dreaded the inevitable re-enactment of the piano scene when we moved on.

Catering to movers, I've always found, is a sensible policy to follow. Offer them snacks—sandwiches and pretzels. Keep cold beer on hand. Bring it out when the day is long and the humidity's high. Don't, however, make the mistake I did, and send your three-year-old tottering over with a can of brew for the man packing china, who, it turns out, is certain sin and beer were invented in the same week.

That fellow was so incensed at the thought of being offered alcohol, and by a child no less, that he slammed a crystal goblet down on the table, grabbed his jacket, and quit on the spot.

Somehow I wasn't surprised. I'd suspected we were going to have trouble with him when he first showed up in the morning. I don't know why. It might have been the fact he was wearing bedroom slippers, and moved with all the alacrity of an arthritic snail. Or it might have been because he kept mumbling, "I hate this damn job." Whatever the reason, we last saw him heading up the street shaking his head and talking to himself.

The actual packing, when the cupboards are emptied and the dishes are sealed in their little padded envelopes, is relatively painless. Oh, there is a trauma or two when you and the children are ordered out of the way and onto the lawn, where the temperature is hovering in the high 90s. And you have a moment of panic when you suspect the crew in the bedroom has sealed up the clothes you were taking with you. But as a rule you're calm and confident. After all, you reason, these folks know what they're doing, and what can really happen within the confines of one truck as it heads from California straight through to Dayton or wherever?

I'll tell you what can happen—what will happen in fact. The truck can leave your house with everyone waving and blowing kisses and shouting thanks. It can then go to the central terminal, where night crews and those employed part time decide there's room for just a few things more. These things belong to someone else, a bachelor perhaps, who lived in a one-room apartment, or a schoolteacher moving in your general direction. There aren't many items, just a couple of cartons, a couch, maybe a bed and nightstand too. It shouldn't be any problem to fit them in. All they have to do is rearrange a bit. So while night falls and a thunderstorm moves in from the west, they unload everything and spread it out in the parking lot. After the rain has stopped, they reload the van, close it up, and head it out.

You of course are blissfully unaware all this is going on. Only when they deliver your goods at your new base will you learn that though seventeen jigsaw puzzles made the trip without so much as losing a piece of sky, the legs of your cinnabar table were snapped off during the reloading process. Only when they haul in someone else's rug and slap it down on your new living room floor, making sure the wine stain is in the center, will you realize your goods had company during the trip.

Right then is usually when I go into a panic. I start racing from room to room, like a relative at the scene of a disaster, looking for belongings I haven't seen yet.

"Hey, Joe," I yell, "did they bring in the cedar chest yet? And what about the toaster? I can't find the toaster."

Of course the movers assure us everything is there. "Look here," they say. "We have a list of all the stuff we packed and loaded, and we're carefully checking it off."

That's a ploy, for the list, every bit as specific as a presidential campaign promise, is full of items marked "stuff from bedroom," "kitchen hardware," or "miscellaneous junk."

Since we never have time to search through everything and discover the handle's been broken off the soup tureen and the wood block prints have inadvertently been left in the van, we use the only weapon we have: Joe's signature. He refuses to sign the delivery sheet that in effect absolves them from everything short of in-transit murder until they've located the few items I know are missing. This upsets movers.

"Come on, lady," they whine, "we gotta get outta here and pick up another load."

"But we're missing a dining room chair," I tell them.

"So—you got seven already. What do you need another for?"

Finally we tell them they're going to be permanent house guests if they don't find that chair, and the foreman stomps off muttering, "Dumb broad. I'll show her."

Minutes later he's back with the chair, a carton containing my entire winter wardrobe, and the box spring for our bed.

The confusion is tripled if perchance you've just come back from a tour overseas, and have had most of your goods in storage while you were gone. For then is when you discover the night watchman at the warehouse spent three years sleeping on your couch during breaks. And then is when you learn they've lost all the legs to your furniture.

We once spent a month eating all our meals off an unhinged kitchen door balanced on a steamer trunk after they lost our legs and the leaves to our table. And I have yet to figure out what to do with my collection of coffee table tops.

But our first move wasn't overseas. It wasn't even across the country. It was only down the street and around the bend a ways.

It was the spring of 1960. The government had decided to remodel the housing area by slapping on a coat of paint and putting in washers, dryers, and air conditioning. It was an action not born entirely out of concern for our welfare. A new Capehart housing facility, complete with sliding doors and patios, had gone up across the highway from the hospital, and though ranking officers in our midst were relocated over there, the rest of us had been told to stand at parade rest, and we were getting surly. So to keep us from marching on the general's quarters, they agreed to update our little village, and as each new section became available they loaded us up and moved us in.

By some enormous stroke of luck Joe qualified for a single-unit three-bedroom house on Hatcher Street, three blocks from our quarters on Nehls. I think it was a reward for having spent eight out of ten Air Force years in Texas, and having been in Wichita Falls since the fall of 1956. Whatever the reason, when Joe got word of the assignment in mid-June, he rushed home and we loaded the children into the stroller and traipsed up to take a look.

The house was in a court of six, arranged like an inverted U, with two on each side, two at the far end, and a huge lawn in the middle. Ours was one of the ones at the end. I could hardly contain myself when I saw it.

"Look Joe," I enthused. "Look at how far we are from the street. That means I won't have to worry so about the children and traffic."

"And look at the size of it," he added.

We peered in through the windows.

"There's even a place for a table in the kitchen. That means we can eat in there, and it will be easier mopping up after Sylvia."

This was a prime consideration, for Sylvia, able to feed herself by now, was not of the crooked finger and tiny morsel school. In keeping with her normal exuberant, uninhibited nature, she attacked her food before it could get the drop on her. Consequently, spaghetti, slapped into submission with the palm of her hand, shot out in all directions. And what didn't catch in the curtains or drape itself on the toaster landed on the floor.

"See"—I pointed—"we can put her feeding table right over there." I took a deep breath. "Did they say when we get to move in?"

"Now, now." Joe tried to temper my impatience. "Don't get so antsy. They said it would be a couple of weeks, at least."

He wasn't far off. The movers came to pick up our stuff on Friday the eighth of July.

Joe and I had already worked out the division of labor. He would supervise the loading and see that the old place passed the traditional moving-out inspection. I would take the children with me up to Hatcher, keep them occupied and out of the way, and then direct the unloading.

I tried not to let on, but I suspected I had the better part of the deal. After all, while he struggled to clean the oven and shine up the broiler racks, all I had to do was wander through the spacious empty rooms and visualize the furniture arrangement. And while he swabbed out behind the refrigerator and the stove, I could meander around the court getting to know the neighbors.

It was lots of fun. Next to us was Ben Fisher; his wife, Joan; his three children—Cathy four, Brad three, and Karen one and a half, and his mother-in-law, Mrs. Barron, or "Mrs. Grandmother," as David and Sylvia would call her. Ben was a SAC bomber pilot, and they'd moved in just three days before.

The house next to theirs was still empty, but John and Betty Blymer lived in the one near the street. I was glad to see their dog Ralph was still alive and still with them. Ralph, a basset hound and dolorous to a fault, had had distemper as a puppy when they lived near us on Nehls, and though he'd finally pulled through, he still had a twitch that made him look like a Civil War veteran tramping over the hills of Gettysburg.

The two families on our side of the court were newcomers to Sheppard. Both had older children, already in school, who couldn't be bothered with two- and three-year-olds. But I could tell from the look in Sylvia's eye that they didn't intimidate her. She'd run with their pack all right. Just as soon as she'd learned to walk.

In the meantime, however, she was content to sit with David and me having a picnic lunch on our new front porch. After lunch, though they both opposed the decision, I put them down for a nap in the cribs Joe and I had brought up early in the morning, and within minutes they were both asleep.

The moving van arrived shortly after one. I ran down to the street to meet it.

"Hi," I trilled. "Good to see you."

The foreman looked at me, looked at the house whence I'd come, and heaved an exhausted sigh.

"That your place up there?" he asked.

"That's it," I told him.

"Hell of a long way," he said, and his tone implied I was at fault.

"Well, I don't know how you can get any closer. It's even farther from the street above."

He shook his head. "Wouldn't you know," he mumbled. Then he turned on his heel. "OK, you guys," he hollered. "Get off your butts and let's get going."

Two other men crawled out of the cab of the van, shuffled to the back, and opened up the doors. I ran back to the house and got ready to receive.

I wasn't ready enough. The next three hours were like being the only policeman directing traffic at the scene of a stampede.

"That box? It goes down the hall and to the right."

"Put the couch pieces here."

"Wait a minute. Doesn't that say kitchen utensils? They go in here."

This of course was my first experience with moving, and fool that I was I expected it to be like the advertisements. I expected handsome starched moving men gently carrying in my precious possessions. I'd swallowed the notion they often break into song while unpacking your bath towels. And I'd believed them when they'd said they carried little Susie's baby doll with them up in the cab so no harm would come to it.

I wasn't prepared for "Hey, lady, do you want I should put your bed together, or can you do it? I got a bad back, you know." I didn't expect "How about if I leave this junk here by the door, and you can put it where you want it later?"

And I certainly didn't think the foreman would walk in and present me with the pieces of a lamp I'd bought only two weeks before and say, "Where do you want me to put these?"

Which is probably why I acted the way I did.

"What do you mean, where do I want you to put these?" I exploded. "That's my new lamp. What did you do to my new lamp?"

"I didn't do nothing," he snarled. "It fell over."

"Fell over? How could it fall over? Wasn't it in a box?"

"Nah, but I put it next to some cushions."

191

"How could you do a dumb thing like that? Didn't you know it would fall?"

"Don't sweat it, lady," he said. "We're insured."

That took some of the wind out of my sails. But my spinnaker billowed once more when he explained being insured meant giving the damagee seven cents a pound for breakage.

"You mean to tell me," I shrilled, eying his jugular vein, "that you've broken my brand-new thirty-five-dollar lamp, and your company's only going to fork over about twenty-eight cents for replacement?"

"That's it," he said. "Now do you want to sign this delivery sheet so we can get out of here?"

Normally I don't fight back. I'm the type who walks around with salesladies' footprints on my back. I apologize for hanging up on obscene phone callers. And I take all the responsibility should someone bump into me or step on my foot. But once in a while, with every tenuous muscle quivering inside of me, my milksopism evaporates, and I let 'em have it.

This was one of those times. I ranted. I raved. I snarled. I threatened. I should have saved my breath. The mover was unmoved.

"Look, lady," he said with a shrug, "you can shout all you want. I'm just following company policy. So why don't you sign this and we'll leave?"

At that point I wouldn't have signed a receipt for a million-dollar gift of emeralds. And since I could hear the children howling in the other room, I decided to make an exit.

"My husband should be here soon," I said as I headed down the hall. "He can sign if he likes. I'm not about to."

Suddenly the mirage of friendly and effusive moving men who did everything but make your beds and tuck you in shimmered once more in front of my eyes. "In the meantime," I snapped, "I'd appreciate it if you all would unpack our kitchen equipment." And I left.

Joe arrived a short time later. He'd been held up waiting for the inspection team, and had he known what awaited him, he might have decided to wait even longer. Thank heavens he didn't. For by the time he strolled in the door, the sound of silverware being dumped on the kitchen table, and the clatter of dishes being slammed into the cupboards was almost deafening. I, my courage drained, cowered in the children's room, wondering what I'd do next.

Luckily I never found out. Joe's arrival brought the mutiny to a halt and before anyone could shout, "Troops dismissed," he'd taken names and addresses, filed breakage forms, signed the delivery sheet, and sent them away.

I minced out of the bedroom and into the kitchen, where he was pouring us both a stiff drink. The counters and the table were piled high with pots, pans, silverware, spatulas, barbecue forks, cake racks, and anything else faintly culinary.

I tried to decide where to start in putting things away, and Joe grabbed Sylvia, who was crawling over to pull herself up and see what was what.

"Well," I said as I gathered up a handful of forks and spoons, and slid them into a drawer, "at least this will make us settle in in a hurry."

Joe shook his head. "Looks that way." He put Sylvia down and headed her into the living room, where David played in an empty packing box. Then he rearranged some dishes in the cupboard.

"Honey?" I said as I handed him a cup I'd found under a pile of dish towels. "Tell me—if three moves equal a fire, what does one equal?"

He picked up one of the pieces of our lamp. "I don't know," he said. "Breaking and entering, I guess."

☆ ★ ☆ 19 ☆ ★ ☆

BEGINNINGS, MIDDLES, AND HOUSEHOLD HELP

I'm a sucker for beginnings. I get rhapsodic about rosebuds, new moons, first chapters, and dawn. I delight in falling snow, football kick-offs, unopened letters, and folded maps. But most of all I love first mornings in a new home. Then is when everything is clean and fresh and perfect. Faults are still looked on as charming idiosyncrasies. Each new discovery is a delight. And for a brief few hours all dreams are possible, all hopes are fulfilled, and life is grand.

With time, reality will point out that the door to the hall closet sticks in damp weather. I'll discover that the kitchen floor shows dirt easily, the back bedroom's cold in winter, there's a crack in the bathroom window, the furnace rattles, and my curtains are all too short. But for the time being all is wonderful.

Joe and I had worked late the night before. We'd lined shelves, put dishes away, and sorted out the silverware drawer. We'd untangled the wire whisk that had woven itself into the wire cake rack. We'd found a place for the cookie sheets and the copper Jell-O molds. And by midnight the kitchen looked as if it might qualify for a small mention in *Better Homes and Gardens* under "Middle-Class Functional but Neat."

Of course the rest of the house was still a collage of packing boxes, wadded newspapers, and coat hangers, but that didn't matter. The morning sun was scheduled to come in the kitchen windows, and that room was ready to greet it.

We both woke up early. Joe, as he always does when I'm counting on his undivided attention, help, and moral support, had made an early appointment to have the car tended to. So when he had showered and shaved and gone off, I got up, got dressed, and tiptoed around the house reveling in all its newness and potential. I even went outside in the back and tried out one of the swings in the neighborhood swing and slide set that by chance was directly behind us.

The morning was still cool, though I could feel heat starting to burn through. As I swung lazily back and forth I listened to the sounds of a Saturday morning: a screen door slamming, a dog barking at nothing in particular, a child's voice rebelling at some injustice. I closed my eyes and tried to memorize every detail. Then I pumped the swing as high as it would go, let it die down, and going inside to the unaccustomed luxury of air conditioning, let the moment pass.

By the time Joe got back I had a pot of fresh coffee ready. The children were still asleep, and since he'd stopped off at a bakery we wallowed in the quiet and feasted on fresh crullers and hot coffee and wondered how life could be so magnificent.

Like all beginnings the magic time ended, and soon the children got up and we got on with the business of sorting, unpacking, arranging the furniture, and hanging the curtains.

David and Sylvia were delighted with their new environs. Their room was large enough so it took her longer to vault her crib across the room so she could shake his bed and pelt him with toys, pacifiers, and an occasional wet diaper. They had a separate playroom where Lincoln log houses could stay intact till she decided to sit on them or try external combustion with a flung block.

David conquered the slide in back immediately and spent hours climbing up, sliding down face first, and then rushing around to climb again. Sylvia aspired to join him. I intervened for as long as I could. On the front porch we gave up before we started on new attempts to grow nasturtiums in the huge square brick planter. Instead we had it filled with a load of sand, and the children's joy was complete.

They sat out there for hours. David dug tunnels and filled up pails and cups and anything else that would hold sand. Sylvia emptied his cups out onto the porch, laughed uproariously when he lectured her, and rubbed sand in her hair. Cathy, Brad, and Karen Fisher came over to play too. There was plenty of room, and between the five of them they built cities—and destroyed them; made pies and cakes—and destroyed them, set up grocery stores—and destroyed them.

They also fought, but no one got excited. Either Mrs. Barron or I simply went over, lifted out the apparent instigator, dusted him or her off, and left the rest to congratulate themselves on being blameless. If that didn't calm things, we set up our pool and lured them all to a cooler sport.

We were excellent playground directors. Justice was swift. Decisions were final. And when all else failed we made lemonade and brought out cookies. Joan was often gone. Unlike me, she was conscientious as an Air Force wife. She did volunteer work at the hospital and committee work for the wives' club. She even offered to serve as decorations chairman for the monthly luncheons. Naturally her offer was accepted. They knew a leader when they saw one.

I knew a leader too, and I knew a persuader. Which is why when they picked a Japanese tearoom theme I found myself being talked into helping make the cherry blossoms.

Joan insisted it was simple and well within my range of expertise, and when she'd appealed to my ever present sense of guilt I capitulated. So she loaded me down with packages of pink crepe paper, wheels of florist wire and tape, and a hurried set of directions; and for weeks I spent every spare moment making cherry blossoms.

I worked on them in the morning when I should have been washing floors and vacuuming. I cut and wired blossoms after I'd put David and Sylvia down for their naps. I took them with me outside when we all relaxed on the lawn in the evening. And late at night while Jack Paar giggled and fawned over Geneviève and the Gabor sisters, I sat in bed and wound and tied and taped and twisted and draped cherry blossoms over Joe's sleeping form.

We must have made thousands. They filled up bowls and bags and shoe boxes. And finally when we could make no more, Joan loaded them up and carried them off to where another persuaded volunteer helped her wire them to large bare branches. I declined to help, but when the lunch was history I heard the decorations were the best the wives' club had ever seen.

Once I'd done my bit and had assuaged my conscience, I felt free to dodge any further requests that I become a clubwoman. It wasn't difficult. Mrs. Barron and I were more than busy with our pint-sized battalion.

When fall came and we had to put the pool away, we held finger painting sessions and brought out the modeling clay. We made butcher paper murals and maps of the land of Oz. And every once in a while we pooled our blocks and rebuilt Old MacDonald's farm.

On Saturday afternoons Joe and David cavorted on the front lawn flying ten-cent balsa planes that looped, glided, and more often than not landed on the roof. I dutifully reported these sessions to Mother in my infrequent letters home. I assured her Sylvia was the funniest and the messiest of all children, and that David was the brightest and the most coordinated. Of course it wasn't exactly true, but Mother, in the best tradition of all grandmothers, believed me.

Fall also stirred Joe into the decision to go after his college degree again. When he'd attended the University of Washington ten years before, sorority girls, bridge tournaments, and functions at the frat house had appealed more than a nine o'clock class in physics, or an evening in the lab. So at the end of his sophomore year he'd bade them farewell before they bade him first.

Now, however, as an officer, a gentleman, a husband, and a father, he decided the time had come to approach life with sobriety and resolution. So in early September he enrolled in night classes at Midwestern University.

I suspected it was a ploy to remove himself from the evening bath scene, and I can't say I blamed him. David and Sylvia loved their bath, but being an active participant in the process was the next best thing to taking a bath yourself. They filled the tub with every toy that would float. They whacked the water with the flat of their hands. They chewed on the washcloths. And once Sylvia mastered the combined art of climbing, walking, and running, she lay in wait till I had my back turned, then slithered out of the tub, scampered down the hall, and fled out the front door. While I raced after her, David made his escape and followed suit.

We three were the main attraction in the neighborhood's evening entertainment, at least we were while the weather stayed warm. Right at seven folks would gather at their front windows and watch me crash out the front door after Sylvia, who was tottering off in one direction, soap suds still clinging to her bare behind, then reverse myself and chase David, who was scurrying the other way. I often got a round of applause, but no one threw money.

Of course when Joe was home I enlisted his help. He wasn't fond of the detail. So when he announced he thought he'd go back to college, naturally I questioned his motives. Who wouldn't? But he assured me he sincerely wanted to get his degree, and who could argue with a noble goal like that?

Joe was good at noble goals. He waved them like banners in front of my snide remarks and protestations. When a fast-talking sergeant who'd always had the yen but never the cash convinced him he should make a sports car, he countered my objections with a noble goal. "I'm only doing it so you can have your own car to drive." And when they both ran into numerous and baffling structural problems and had to abandon the project, he waved his banner and told me, "But honey, you said you didn't like having me gone so much."

This time when I grumbled at being left alone in the evenings and ignored on weekends while he studied the causes of the French Revolution, he hauled out his noble goal, looked crestfallen, and said, "But I'm only trying to get a better education."

Classes were three nights a week. Joe left around six-thirty and got back shortly after ten. While he was gone, I bathed, rocked, read stories, and put the children to bed two or three times. Then I entertained myself with mounds of unfolded diapers, unironed uniforms, and *Route 66* or *Hawaiian Eye*. Sometimes Joan came over, and we had coffee and talked. Sometimes I called up old neighbors from Nehls, though most had either gone back to civilian life or had been reassigned.

At ten I turned on the late news and waited for Joe. I always heard him coming. Normally after he'd parked the car down at the street, he approached the house with all the stealth of an Arab in tennis shoes tiptoeing through the sand. At night, however, he slammed doors, coughed, whistled, and sang as he came up the walk.

He had to. His life was in danger. Penny Lambright, who lived in the corner house across the street was out to get him. She was out to get everyone. Her husband, an instructor pilot, was gone a lot, and the moment his plane disappeared into the proverbial wild blue yonder, she heard parades of prowlers, burglars, rapists, and murderers skulking about in the shrubbery. Sometimes all Jack had to do was get in his car and go mail a letter, and while he was gone escaped mental patients rattled her windows and hid in her bushes.

It got so the Air Police were in our neighborhood more than they were at the guardhouse. For a while we dismissed Penny's apprehensions as simple paranoia. Then one day Joan came home and told us Penny said she kept a loaded gun in her dresser drawer and was ready to use it.

After that Joe took no chances. "Hell," he told me the first night when I asked why he'd made so much noise, "I could almost feel her there behind the curtains drawing a bead on the back of my head. You bet I'm going to make noise. It's better than getting a bullet between the ears. That woman's crazy and I'm not about to upset her."

"Oh, come on, Joe," I scoffed. "She's not crazy. She simply has a vivid imagination."

But vivid imagination or no, the uneasiness was catching, and soon other wives started seeing shadowy figures in the dark. Meg Anderson, down the street, claimed she saw a Peeping Tom one night staring in her bathroom window. Dolly Flannery swore she saw him too.

"At least I think it was a Peeping Tom," she said one day over coffee. "I looked out my kitchen window, and a dark form ducked around the corner of our neighbor's house."

Joan and Mrs. Barron took no chances. With Ben away as much as he was, they claimed they weren't about to be murdered in their beds.

"But Peeping Toms don't murder, they just sneak furtive glances and fall off of roofs," I assured them one night when Joan invited me over to show me her array of bolts and locks and chains. "Besides," I added, "how do we know this isn't another of Penny's phantom criminals?"

"We don't," Joan said, "but I'm not about to take any chances, and you'd be smart to lock up too."

I knew I would, but somehow I couldn't get that enthused. I was pregnant again, and as I told Joe, "If that poor devil is desperate enough to look in our window and feast his eyes on this ungainly form, he deserves what he sees."

Apparently the fellow agreed with me. For while everyone on the block reported a sighting or two, I never heard so much as a twig snap outside our place. It got so I was ashamed to admit it though.

Finally Penny's husband was reassigned, and she packed up her assortment of night visitors and moved to Guam, where, I imagine, she produced a new set in an Oriental motif.

Once she'd gone, folks lost interest, and the sightings dropped off till they were almost nonexistent.

I remember the day she left. It was the same day her cleaning lady, Mrs. Evard, agreed to come to my house and muck out our stalls once a week, and I was terrified. I'd never had a cleaning lady before. Not that I disapproved. I didn't. I was the first to admit I had neither the talent nor the inclination for domesticity, and I gladly welcomed any help in that line. But like the proverbial cartoon character, I wanted her to deem me worthy.

So I'd been up since dawn. I'd made the beds, dressed the children, fed them, and done the dishes. I picked up the clutter in the living room, wiped off the bathroom mirror, rolled up the toothpaste tube, located the cap in the corner on the floor and put it on. I'd put the shower curtain in the wash in hopes I could hang it back mildew free before Mrs. Evard arrived. I'd had the children pick up their toys and put them in the toy chest.

I'd even swept the kitchen floor, and all so I could be casual and controlled when she came.

She arrived about nine. I could tell right away I didn't measure up. It might have been my clothes. I was dressed rather casually in an old skirt and blouse. It might have been the coffee I offered. It was strong, and when she made a face I had to heat up some water to dilute it. Or it might have been that I wasn't apologetic enough for the condition of the house. I certainly tried to be. After a while my witless babblings nauseated even me. But Mrs. Evard was unimpressed.

"I break at ten-thirty," she said in a tone that made me wonder why she was cleaning houses when she obviously should have been a squadron commander. "I eat lunch at noon—sandwich, coffee, and maybe some canned fruit or cookies. No spicy foods though." She patted her stomach. "They don't set well with me."

"Of course. Of course," I slathered.

"One other thing," she added lest I interrupt her ground rules with an insignificant request of my own such as she get to work. "Yes?"

"I don't stay past three. My bus leaves at three-ten exactly, and I'm not about to miss it for nothing."

"Fine." I paused, giving her an in for any more instructions. Then, when she had none, I hauled out a sheet of paper. "Now let me just show you what I'd like done today." I ran through the chores I had in mind, trying to keep my apologies to a minimum. Then I let her get on with it and busied myself elsewhere.

It wasn't easy. For one thing I had trouble finding things to do. I couldn't sit down at the kitchen table, pour myself another cup of coffee, and thumb through the paper. Not with her right there scrubbing the appliances. I certainly couldn't go next door and leave her with the housework and the children too. And I didn't dare tell David to bring out his blocks so we could make a tower, because once she'd cleaned the living room I could sense she would not be pleased watching us mess it up again.

201

Finally I put on the children's coats and took them for a walk. We went down to the street and watched Peggy's movers toss her furniture around for a while. Then we wandered around the block, stopping to pick up each pebble, to say hello to each dog, and to examine each crack in the sidewalk. When we got home we went up to the swings, and David showed Sylvia how to climb the ladder on the slide and go down face first.

Then we went inside for lunch. I knew the sandwich—bologna, lettuce, and mayonnaise—wasn't to her liking when I saw her scrape some mayonnaise into the sink. I think the coffee was still too strong and the peaches were too spicy, but finally the meal ended anyway and I put the children down for their nap.

The afternoon dragged even more slowly. I couldn't let Mrs. Evard think I was one of those slovenly housewives who sit around watching soap operas, so I gave up *As the World Turns* and got out some ironing instead. It was quite a sacrifice. I hate ironing as much as I hate scrubbing toilets. I think she could tell.

"Oh, my, you got a load there," she said when I brought out the basket that was so full the stack of shirts on top teetered and threatened to fall.

"Oh, this," I fluttered. "It's just that I did a lot of washing yesterday."

"Um-hm."

I could tell she didn't believe me. Why should she? It was a lie. But I stuck to my story and virtuously grabbed a shirt, sprinkled it and started to iron. By quarter to three, when I heard the first sounds of Sylvia beating her head against the wall, I'd worked my way down below the rim. I felt as if I'd been at it for days.

"Mrs. Evard," I said, as I unplugged the iron and put it up out of the way to cool, "I'm going to get the children up now. Since it's almost three, why don't you finish what you're doing and then you can go." I put her check on the kitchen counter. Then I fled down the hall calling out my thanks as I went.

By the time I had them up and dressed she was gone. Obviously she'd worked till the last minute, for a bucket of dirty water was still in the middle of the kitchen floor. I got it before Sylvia did. There was a wet rag on the coffee table, and I grabbed it before

Sylvia could whisk it up and fling it at David. She beat me to the cleanser left on the edge of the tub, however, and it took me twenty minutes to wipe down the walls and rinse the grit off the floor.

I was still at it when Joe came home.

"Hi kids," I heard him say when the children greeted him at the door. "Where's your mommy?"

"In there," David answered. "She's in there, cleaning up after the cleaning lady."

Y'ALL COME BACK
NOW, HEAH?

The official orders came on the tenth of March, 1961.

To: Captain Joseph R. Combs, Jr.
   3762 School Sq (62-T)
   This is to notify you of your selection for permanent change of
station to 1125 USAF Field Activities Gp, Wright-Patterson AFB,
Ohio, with permanent duty station, Air Tech Intelligence Liaison Office, Det 4, Tokyo, Japan, reporting in July, AFSC 8044. You will
be placed on TDY to 1125 USAF Fld Act Gp for 30 days prior to
departure for overseas . . .

"What does it all mean?" I asked.

It was dinnertime. I was stirring up a white sauce, wanting to
leave it be so I could concentrate on savoring every detail, but not
daring to, lest it lump.

"Tell me exactly what's going to happen."

I already knew the basics. We'd both been holding our breath
on this one for weeks. Ever since the night Joe got a call from
Colonel Samper, who was in Washington, D.C., on official business.

The colonel, it turned out, had been in a meeting earlier that day where he'd learned there was soon to be an opening for an intelligence officer in Tokyo, and he was calling to see if Joe would be interested in the job.

He could have saved his money.

"Are you kidding?" Joe shouted as I sat by wondering what on earth he was talking about. "I'd jump at the chance."

"Then put in a request for transfer," he was told, "tomorrow—first thing."

"I will, sir. Yes, sir. Thank you, sir." Joe's face beamed. "I'll even go in early."

"Go in early for what?" I asked after he'd hung up.

"To apply for a transfer to Tokyo."

"Really?"

"Really." He paused for a minute while I shivered with delight. "But don't get too excited," he warned. "I'm just applying. There's no guarantee I'll get the assignment."

"Oh, I know," I said, already planning side trips to Kyoto, Nara, and Hong Kong. "I know. Nothing is certain till the orders are in your hand."

"That's right, and don't you forget it."

I didn't, but now the orders were there, right on our kitchen table, staring us in the face, and like a colt let free in a meadow, I galloped through the thought of it all, whirled around, and trotted back to gallop through it again.

"Still I'm confused," I said, stirring automatically but paying no attention to what I was doing. "What do they mean you've been selected for a permanent change of station to Wright-Pat?"

"It's simple. I go to Wright-Pat for indoctrination, to get an idea of what I'll be doing."

"Oh. How long is that?"

"About three weeks to a month."

"What do we do in the meantime?"

"Well I was thinking about that. As I see it, since you're due to have the baby at the end of June, the best thing, probably, would be for you and the children to leave here in May and go up to Bainbridge and stay with your folks and have the baby up there. I'll join you as soon as I can."

205

"Will you get there before the baby's born?"

"I should. I'm supposed to leave here around the middle of May. I'll drive up to Dayton, stay in the BOQ till, say, the middle of June, then drive west. Unless you're terribly early, that should get me there in plenty of time."

"But when, then, do we leave for Japan?"

"We don't. At least you and the children don't—not right away."

"Why not?"

"The Air Force won't let you travel till the baby's at least ten weeks old."

I stopped stirring. "Why not?"

"I don't know. They just won't, that's all."

"But that means we won't get there till sometime in September. I don't know if I can wait."

"You'll have to wait." Joe handed me a drink and moved the white sauce off the burner, lest it scorch. "They aren't authorizing concurrent travel. Besides," he said, as he dumped some grated cheese in and stirred it around, "you'll be so busy, what with the new baby and all, that the time will pass before you know it."

"Perhaps." I poured the sauce over some potatoes, put them in a casserole, and slid it into the oven. Then I sat down at the kitchen table. "Now," I said, anxious to get on to subject two. "What do we do about all our belongings? I mean, do we have them all sent? I'm going to need a lot of stuff with me, just to make it through the summer."

"Calm down," he said. "It'll all work out. We have to put some of the stuff, the furniture mainly, in permanent storage."

I shuddered, but Joe held up his hand. "We have to," he said. "They only ship so many pounds of household goods per person. Besides, all the housing overseas is furnished." He paused to make sure that settled that. Then he continued. "So, we have the stuff in storage. Then there's another batch. This includes clothes, dishes, pots, pans, and such. This they pack and hold till we get our housing assignment. Then they ship it on to us. The third set are the belongings you take with you to Bainbridge. These you deliver up to Paine Field, just before you leave, and the transportation people send them on from there."

206

I shook my head. "Sure sounds complicated to me."

"It isn't really. The main thing for you to remember is that you and the children will wing your way up to Bainbridge when I leave for Ohio. Then while you're lazing about digging clams and having fresh strawberries, I'll be whipping through my indoctrination classes. When they're through I'll drive like a maniac to be at your side for the birth of our third offspring. Then at the end of July I'll leave for Tokyo, and you all will follow in September. See?" He gave a magic wave of his hand. "Nothing to it. Now if you'll excuse me I'll go find the children and tell them to get washed up for dinner."

I got up and went to put some carrots on to cook. September, I thought. Come September and I'll be cooking carrots in Tokyo. It seemed too good to be true. Somehow I'd resigned myself to being in the land of hush puppies and black-eyed peas forever, and now here I was about to go to Tokyo. I wonder if I'll learn to make sukiyaki and tempura, I thought idly.

That was the last idle thought I had. From then on things got frantic.

First, of course, we all had to get our shots—cholera, typhoid, tetanus, and polio. Every Friday morning up at the shot clinic at the hospital we joined the other men and their families who were headed overseas.

It wasn't a joyous occasion. For after the first "This won't hurt a bit, young man," David and Sylvia saw through the medical palaver. Of course it was going to hurt, and they were going to have a nice long wait in line remembering just how much. So every Friday they refused to get out of the car. They dragged their feet and dawdled as we walked over to the clinic. And they cowered behind me and hid in the folds of my skirt while we waited.

It might not have been so difficult had they whisked us in and whisked us out. But they don't whisk in the Air Force. They line you up, around the block preferably, and tell you to stop complaining. They'll be with you as soon as they can.

So we stood in line, and while the other children shrieked and howled and bolted for the door, I tried to distract ours with wonderful tales of how we were bound to meet the emperor and be invited for tea as soon as we got to Japan. They didn't believe me. They didn't distract either, and by the time we'd worked our way through typhus, paratyphoid, and a smallpox booster, merely the sight of a white coat sent them off screaming.

Days at home were spent sifting, sorting, and throwing away. It was a hassle when it came to the toys. All day long I'd sort. Trucks and games went into the hold baggage. Stuffed animals and story books came with us. Lincoln logs and blocks went into the hold baggage. Sand shovels and buckets came with us.

No sooner would I get one box ready than David or Sylvia would wander in, paw through my choices, and make an impassioned plea for clemency for a dump truck or a puppet, wailing, "Save it, Mommy. Don't throw it away."

"I'm not throwing anything away," I'd try to explain. "I'm just packing these up to send to Japan so they'll be waiting for you when you get there."

They didn't buy that, and when I wasn't looking, they dug into the boxes, dragged out sudden favorites, and piled them in their cribs, where they figured they'd be safe. It wasn't long before the cribs looked like cages three and four in the Ringling Brothers parade, and there was hardly any room for the children. So I readjusted my schedule and sorted toys at night.

During the day I sifted through the rest of our belongings. At first it was hard.

"I simply can't throw this sweater out," I'd say to myself. "After all it's hardly worn, and who knows when I'll need an extra sweater?"

"You already have three heavy cardigans," myself would reply. "Besides, this color green makes you look as if you've been seasick since November."

"But Mother gave it to me when I first went away to college."

"And how many times have you worn it since then?"

"Not many, true. In fact I think the last time was when I changed a tire in the summer of 'fifty-four."

"I rest my case. Now put it in the Goodwill bag and forget it."

After a while I stopped arguing and got into the swing of it.

"Goodbye, cologne," I'd chant, tossing out a bottle of something I'd had since high school that smelled like essence of boiled turnips.

"Good luck, broken sunglasses, 1959 Smithsonian calendar, and Vicar's old water dish."

"And you, lilac shoes once dyed to match a nylon net formal, go haunt someone else with your potential. And while you're at it, take this nauseating pair of mustard yellow gloves with you."

"Boy," Joan said one day when she came over to see how I was doing, "you're really going at this with a vengeance."

"You bet I am, and it feels wonderful. I can't tell you how long I've hated some of this stuff. This for instance." I hauled out a box of carefully smoothed and folded Christmas paper. "Every year I think, Oh, dear, I can't throw this away. I might need it sometime. I even found a birthday card from our insurance man in one of my drawers. Boy, that went out in a hurry." I tossed the paper, box and all, into my garbage carton.

"I know what you mean," she said, reaching into the box to take out and thumb through a government booklet called *You and Your New Baby.* "You can tell you've finally made it as an Air Force wife when you learn to throw things away." She pitched the pamphlet back. "I didn't really get into the spirit of the whole thing till we'd moved twice. Now, though, I'm callous as hell. I don't even keep the children's drawings, though Mother tries to convince me I'll want them someday."

"I know what you mean." I pulled out another drawer, set it on the bed, and started to go through it. "But luckily I don't have time to agonize over some of this stuff. I just have to throw and hope I won't regret it."

I certainly didn't have time. Whereas the original plan had been for the children and me to head west the same day Joe took off for Wright-Patterson, my doctor ruled otherwise.

"I want you out of here by the first of May," he said. "I want you safely settled a good two months before this baby's due."

"But why?"

"Because this is your third child, and knowing you, you'll probably have it early. Besides," he added, "airlines won't let pregnant women travel if they're closer to delivery than six weeks."

"Is that true?" I asked Joe later when I told him what Dr. Maxwell had said.

"Yes. I think it is."

"But what if I don't go on a plane?" I said.

I'd been dreading the thought of eight hours in the sky in the company of a two- and three-year-old ever since we got our orders. Somehow I didn't look forward to having them scamper off in the Denver airport with me lumbering after them. I didn't relish the idea of chasing them up and down the aisle of the plane either, especially during the traditional "slight turbulence" over Amarillo, and I had nightmares about little meals on little trays with little glasses of milk tipping over.

"What do you mean, what if you don't go on a plane?"

"What if we take the train?"

"The train?"

"Yeah. We could get a roomette, even have our meals there if necessary. Do you think the Air Force would allow that?"

"Sure, I know they would, mainly because it's cheaper. But you know you'd be traveling for three days and two nights, and that's a long time compared to a short flight."

"Oh, I don't mind. I love trains. Besides, it would be less trouble in the long run. We could go up to the dome cars and watch the scenery. The children could play in the roomette. They could take naps. If we went to the dining car, and I hear they're dome cars too now, we'd have a table, and a table's easier to work with than those airline things."

Joe's eyes glazed over. I could see he wanted to come too. Finally he spoke. "Why not?" he said. "I think it's a great idea. It will even save you the trouble of having anything shipped up to Bainbridge since you can take it all with you."

So it was settled. We'd go by train. Joe notified Transportation. They ground out assorted orders, including a set that would eventually take the children and me to Tokyo. They specified what would "commence on or before . . ." They warned what would happen "not later than . . ." They noted succinctly "expenses are chargeable to 5723500.002 P537.01 S503725 2100. CIC: 45 248 5376 503725. 5723500 P537.01 S503725 2200." And they told me what actions were expected of me "at earliest practicable date." Then they handed me my ticket, wished me "Bon voyage, sir," and signed themselves,

"Sincerely, SO AB-455, Hq Sheppard Technical Training Ctr (ATC), Sheppard AFB, Texas."

With that taken care of, I had an entire two weeks to pack for a four-month stay at Mother's and Daddy's, to say goodbye to all my friends, who would have given anything to be in my place, and to finish getting ready for the movers.

Joe, in this new turn of events, had drawn moving day detail. He wasn't thrilled with the prospect, but I assured him the division of labor was more than equitable.

"After all," I reminded him, "you have only one horrible day with the cardboard carton and glass packing set. Then you're free as a bird. You can play golf, go to the movies, swim, whatever you want. I, on the other hand, will still have children to feed, clothes to wash, toys to pick up—if I can manage to bend that far—and meals to cook."

Secretly I didn't mind at all. Anything was better than facing the movers and watching them play volleyball with our china cups. But I wasn't about to admit it.

I took one day off to say all my goodbyes. I went down to the symphony office and rode up in the elevator with the buffalo man, who remarked I seemed to be in a continual state of pregnancy. Tom was there, shuffling through papers as usual, and he flattered me, I think, saying things hadn't been the same since I left. I told him to behave himself and find some nice girl and settle down.

Dr. Kohary was on tour back east, so I missed him. I did leave a note for him with Tom, however, even though I knew full well he'd probably lose it or inadvertently throw it out.

Next I drove out to Lettie's. Aunt Mulie peered through the curtains when I knocked, then skittered back to the kitchen, where I heard her jabbering, "It's her, Lettie. She's back. The naked lady's back."

Lettie was doing laundry as usual, and she looked a little older and a little tired. "But don't worry, hon," she assured me. "With Junior in school all day, and Elwood gone in the mornings, it's almost peaceful."

"I imagine it is."

"Grandpa O died, you know," she said. "Last fall."

"Oh, Lettie. I'm sorry."

"Don't be. He wasn't in no pain. Just one morning he didn't get up, and when Pa went in to check, he was dead."

I hugged her as much as my girth would allow. "Take care of yourself," I said. "We think of you often. We always have, even though we never managed to get back and see you much."

"You too, girl," she said, and for a minute I was afraid she might cry. I should have known better. "Now get on with you." She laughed. "And when you get to Japan," she added as I went out the door, "don't eat no raw fish or pickled monkey brains."

"I won't," I said. "And tell Aunt Mulie the naked lady's gone."

"OK. Goodbye."

I was going to stop by Saint Mary's and see if either Alden or Leslie was home, but suddenly as I drove by the wedding with all its frills seemed terribly dim and long ago. So I merely slowed up, glanced at the church, and headed home.

"You know, Joe," I said that night as we were getting ready for bed, "it's funny. I'm dying to leave. I can hardly wait to see everyone at home, and then be in Japan. But somehow it seems we're always saying goodbye to special people. And I know that in spite of all our good and sincere intentions, we'll lose touch and forget to write and probably never see each other again. Even if we do meet, we'll be different people then, in fact virtual strangers."

"I know." He put his arm around my shoulder. "But you may be surprised. Air Force friendships, I've found, are usually stronger than most."

I woke up early the day we left. I needn't have. The train wasn't due to go till three that afternoon. But I couldn't sleep. My mind was racing.

Let's see, did I remember to pack David's extra jacket and some aspirin? . . . I better get those diapers in the wash right away, so they'll be dry in time. . . . I wonder if I should take some snacks along for the children. . . . Where did I put that pocketbook I bought the other day? . . . Lord, what if I forget my ticket? . . . Joe had it last night. . . . He said he wanted to check to see when I get into Portland. . . . Did he put it back in my purse?

Finally I got up. The children and Joe were still asleep, and I showered as quietly as I could. Then I tiptoed into the kitchen and put on a pot of coffee.

I'm going to miss this house, I thought as I sat at the table and listened to the coffee bubble and perk. We haven't even been here a year. I wonder what the house in Tokyo will be like? Joan said a friend of hers lived off base for a year before they could get housing. That might be fun. She also said everyone there has full-time maids.

I reveled in the thought of someone else doing the dishes, cleaning out the refrigerator, and ironing Joe's uniforms, and speculated as to whether they'd have to leave to catch a bus at three.

"I wonder how long they'll let us stay there," I said out loud.

"Stay where?" Joe was standing in the doorway with a towel wrapped around him.

"What?"

"You said, 'I wonder how long they'll let us stay.' "

"Oh"—I laughed—"I was just thinking of Tokyo and how they say everyone has full-time maids, and I wondered if we could wangle it so you could spend the rest of your career there."

He shook his head. "Not hardly," he said. "It's like what you always say about the commissary. Once they find out you're attached to something, they move heaven and earth to do away with it."

"You're probably right." I poured myself some coffee. "You want some," I asked, "or do you want to get dressed first?"

"I'll wait," he said. "Say, what time are we due at Joan's?"

"Ten."

"OK."

Joan had invited us all over for a farewell breakfast, but there was lots of time. When the children got up I gave them some juice and a piece of toast to tide them over. Then I stripped their beds and put in the first load of wash. I would have liked to strip them too. It seemed the perfect way to keep them clean till it was time to go, but I didn't want to enhance our reputation as a preschool nudist camp.

Once we got over to Joan's, the time flew. We ate, had some champagne punch, and played remember when.

"Remember when we made the hundred thousand cherry blossoms?"

"Remember when your mother and the children locked themselves out of the house and we couldn't find you?"

"Remember the kite flying competition we had, when Brad's broke its string and got away?"

"I think he cried for two hours straight."

Finally it was time to go. I tried to say goodbye, to say thank you, and we'll keep in touch, but Joan stopped me.

"Go," she said. "Go help Joe load the car."

"But . . ."

"Now."

I went, and by the time I had the children washed and combed and had whipped the last of the diapers out of the dryer and stuffed them in my suitcase, Joe had taken everything down to the car, and Joan and her children had gone off to the commissary.

We got to the station with plenty of time to spare. Joe checked most of our luggage straight through, then helped us carry the rest aboard. The children were delighted with the roomette. They checked out the bathroom, pulled down the sink, climbed into the chairs, and peered down the passageway.

Joe enthralled them with an explanation of where the beds were hidden, and I showed them how to put the table up.

Then it was two minutes to three.

"Now you call me," Joe said, "just as soon as you get there."

"I will."

"And take care of yourself."

"You too."

"And don't worry. I'll be there before you know it."

"I know. . . . Good luck with the movers."

He stood on the platform outside the window and waved till the conductor pulled up the steps and the train started to move forward. David and Sylvia pressed their noses against the window and watched till they couldn't see him any more.

I looked out at the flat countryside as we picked up speed. In the distance the horizon looked rusty.

"Is Daddy going home now?" David asked.

"That's right," I said, "and he'd better hurry, 'cause it looks as if a dust storm is due to hit in about twenty minutes."